AF560683

REVENUE FREE LAND GRANTS IN MUGHAL INDIA

Revenue Free Land Grants in Mughal India

AWADH REGION IN THE SEVENTEENTH AND EIGHTEENTH CENTURIES (1658–1765)

JIGAR MOHAMMED

MANOHAR
2002

First published 2002

ISBN 81-7304-420-1

Published by
Ajay Kumar Jain for
Manohar Publishers & Distributors
4753/23 Ansari Road, Daryaganj
New Delhi 110 002

Typeset by
Kohli Print
Delhi 110 051

Printed at
Rajkamal Electric Press
Delhi 110 033

To my teacher
Professor S.N. SINHA

Contents

Preface

During the Mughal period the land revenue was distributed among the persons of different socio-political backgrounds. The Mughal emperor assigned revenue of a particular area to a noble in lieu of his salary. Such revenue assignment were known as *jagir.* Land revenue of some areas were meant for the expenditure of the Mughal emperor, such assignement was known as *khalisa.* Persons of religious background and needy were assigned revenue free land known as *milk, aimma* and *madad-i-maash.* In Mughal period religious institutions received grant support from the masses as well as state. The persons of religious background had established their separate identity in the society. The religious group, either of Hindu or Muslim community, were backed by the society. They also received considerable political patronage. Since the people of this group were recognized as 'pious men', they were not expected to do any menial work. Consequently state extended financial support to them. Since ancient period it was general practice to assign revenue free lands to religious persons so that they could survive and serve society without any economic pressure. However, during Mughal period, particularly from Akbar's regin the scope of assignment of revenue free land grant was widened. The nature and method of assignment of these grants were given a definite shape and separate department was established to look after this work. The categories of the grant holders were well determined.

In Mughal India the practice of revenue free land grants was known by different terms such as *sayurghal madad-i-maash,* and *aimma.* However, *madad-i-maash* became a more popular term for revenue free land grants. The conditions of the assignement of *madad-i-maash* lands were liberalized so as to help a larger number of people. Though the bulk of the grants were given to the *ulema* (men of the religious class), the destitute were also considered for such assignments. Several rules and regulations were made about *madad-i-maash* grants, which remained important aspects of social, economic and political life of the region.

In Awadh *madad-i-maash* holders occupied an important place in the socio-economic set-up of the suba. They had a monoploy over the religio-judicial offices. A large number of grant documents of Awadh are available for the period of late seventeenth and the eighteenth centuries which help in the study of the *madad-i-maash* grants as a system. Some articles have been written on this aspect, however no detailed study has been made regarding the working of this system as an important part of the Mughal administration. Aspects like concentration and distribution, the role of grant holders in society, their position and their relations with other landed classes of the suba, need a detailed study. The present study is primarily based on my Ph.D. thesis through this study an attempt has been made to study the various aspects of the assignment of the *madad-i-maash* grants under the Mughals. The study of this important institution of the Mughal administrative set-up unfolds many interesting informations and details which may help in appreciating the impact of this system on the socio-religious and political life at the local level.

This study is primarily based on original grant documents and other sources. A large number of Allahabad Documents, preserved at Uttar Pradesh State Archives, Allahabad, and Acquired Documents, preserved at National Archives of India, Delhi, have been consulted. Besides, the Mughal chronicles and secondary sources have been consulted. The translations of the Mughal chronicles have been verified by the original texts.

I am thankful to Prof. S.N. Sinha, Department of History, Jamia Millia Islamia, New Delhi for his valuable suggestions and guidance for the completion of the present study. I must express my gratitude to Professor Mushirul Hasan who extended every possible help to me regarding my research work. Whenever I felt any problem in my research work he tried to solve them. I have greatest pleasure in thanking Dr. Muzaffar Alam, Professor, Centre for Historical Studies, Jawaharlal Nehru, University, for his help in various ways. He drew my attention to many useful documents concerning my research work. I am thankful to my teachers Dr. R.A. Khan, Dr. Mujeeb Ashraf, Dr. Inayat Ali Zaidi, Dr. Sunita Zaidi and Dr. Azizuddin Husain for their help and valuable advice. Dr. Azizuddin Husain took keen interest in my research work. They drew my attention towards some useful materials related to my research work.

JIGAR MOHAMMED

Abbreviations

Allahabad Doc.	:	Allahabad Documents, Uttar Pradesh State Archives, Allahabad
IHR	:	*Indian Historical Review*
PIHC	:	Proceedings of Indian History Congress
PIHRC	:	Proceedings of Indian Historical Record Commission
NAI	:	Acquired Documents, National Archives of India, Delhi

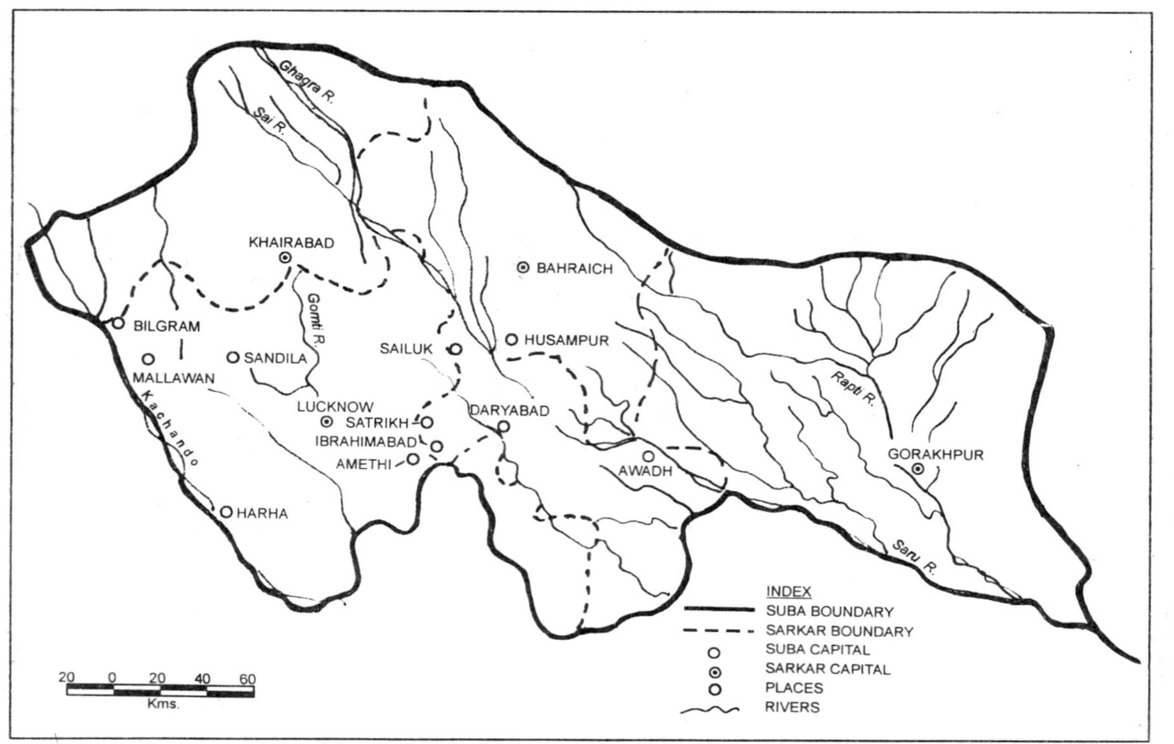

SUBA OF AWADH: SOME IMPORTANT CENTRES OF *MADAD-I-MAASH* GRANTS BASED ON *MUGHAL ATLAS*

CHAPTER 1

Introduction

In ancient times Awadh was known as Ajoydhya.[1] In the seventh century Ayodhya constituted the central portion of the empire of Harsha. It then became a province under the sultans of Delhi. Awadh, occupied the major part of the Gangetic plain in the Ganga-Jamuna Doab region[2] but it is difficult to define the exact boundaries of Awadh, due to varying political situations.

In 1580, when Akbar reorganized his empire into twelve subas, Awadh was one of them.[3] According to Abul Fazl the length of the suba was 135 *kos* and its breadth was 115 *kos.*[4] It was bounded by the mountains in the north, the suba of Bihar was in the east, the suba of Allahabad in the north and that of Agra in the west.[5]

THE LANDSCAPE

The chief rivers of the suba were the Saru—(Sarju), the Ghagra (Gogra), the Sai and Godi (Gomti).[6] The Sarju and Ghagra were the major rivers of Awadh and these two were chiefly responsible for inundations.[7] The Sarju flows from Bahraich and forms the boundary with Nepal for a few miles.[8] The Ghagra starts in the north-west of Bahraich from Kheri and Sitapur. It is joined the Chauka river at Bahramghat and passing the then sarkar of Awadh, separated it for some 50 miles of its course from the sarkar of Gorakhpur.[9] The Gomti flows through Lucknow and Sultanpur. The Sai flows through Kheri in the sarkar of Khairabad.[10]

The soils of the suba could be classified into three categories:

1. *Matiyar* or clay soil;
2. *Domat, Doras* or loam soil. This soil was mixture of clay and ·land; and
3. *Bhur* or light soil.[11]

The suba consisted of two-third of *domat* or loam soil, while of the remaining one-third, one-half was *matiyar* and the other wars *bhur* or light sandy soil.[12] The soil of southern portion of Awadh was light.[13] Between the Gomti and Ganga the soil is sandy and called *usar.*[14] In this part the light arable soil is found between 2 or 3 miles in diameter of the *usar* soil.[15] The richest soil in the south of Awadh was found near Jais, Rampur and Manikpur.[16]

Irrigation in Awadh was by lifting water from rivers, wells and tanks. River water was raised with the use of leather bags,[17] baskets,[18] and *duglas*[19] at multi-level heights.[20]

A large part of the suba was irrigated by the Sarju and Ghagra.[21]

There were two devices for lifting water from the wells in Awadh suba, the *dhenklis* (wooden scoops),[22] and the *charas*.[23]

Tanks were a common source of irrigation in the suba of Awadh. During the Mughal period, almost every village of the suba had a tank—masonry or non-masonry—dug every year or two.[24] Non-masonry tanks were usually used for irrigation. Generally a tank supplied water for 20 *bighas* of land,[25] and remained serviceable for 50 to 60 years.[26] The water was raised from tanks by means of *duglas* or swing baskets.[27]

The climate of the suba is good. Summer and winter are usually temperate.[28] It is very hot and dry from April to June, very hot and moist from July to October and bright, clean and pleasant during the rest of the year.[29] The average annual rainfall is from 36 to 40 inches.[30]

Like other parts of northern India, the province of Awadh was a double-crop area with *rabi* (spring) and *kharif* (autumn). The *rabi* crops included different types of food grains, oil seeds, and some cash crops.[31] *Kharif* crops included sugar cane, rice, pulses and cash crops.[32]

Both *rabi* and *kharif* crops indicate that in the suba food grain, pulses and sugar cane were sown on a large scale. Cash crops like cotton and indigo had poor yields in the suba. These crops were sown in a small tracts of land of the suba.

ADMINISTRATIVE DIVISIONS

The suba of Awadh was divided into five sarkars,[33] Awadh, Gorakhpur, Bahraich, Khairabad, and Lucknow. These sarkars were further divided into parganas.[34] The sarkar of Awadh contained 21 parganas or mahals, Gorakhpur had 24,[35] Bahraich 11,[36] Khairabad 22,[37] and Lucknow 55 parganas. Thus the total number of parganas in the suba of Awadh was 133.[38] The parganas were further divided into villages. The village was the smallest unit for the assessment of land revenue. The quality and fertility of soil was the main consideration for revenue assessment.

THE POLITICAL CONDITION OF AWADH (1658–1765)

Each suba was placed under the administrative control of a subedar, who was called *nazim* or *sipahsalar*.[39] The main functions of the subedar were to collect the revenue, preserve law and order, maintain roads and communications and ensure a minimum of military aid to the emperor.

From the sixteenth to the seventeenth century, politically Awadh was well organized. The Mughal emperor did not face any major political crisis in Awadh. The zamindars of Awadh enjoyed fairly important political position at the local level.

However, after the death of Aurangzeb, fast political changes took place in the court of Delhi. When the central authority became weak, the chieftains of the different parts of the country tried to assert their independence. The chieftains of Awadh also tried to defy the central authority. Awadh virtually became independent under Saadat Khan,[40] who was appointed as governor of Awadh in 1722. Although Saadat Khan acknowledged the supremacy of the Mughals, in practice he was an independent power.

Saadat Khan, the first Nawab of Awadh, found the suba with a number of chieftains, exercising independent power in their respective areas. The first task before Saadat Khan was therefore to establish his supremacy over those deficient chieftains of the suba. The powerful among those chieftains were Mohan Singh, raja of Tiloi (in the present Rae Bareli district). The rajas of Bansi, Rasulpur and Binayakpur in Basti, Chattradhari Singh Sombansi, raja of Pratapgarh, Chet Rai Bais of Baiswara, Raja Dutta Singh of Gonda, Raja Narain Singh of Balrampur in the Gonda district.[41]

Besides these Rajput cheifs, the Shaikhzadas were also powerful in the areas of Lucknow, from the time of Akbar, and during his reign Shaikh Abdul Rahim, an impecunious nobleman of Bijnor was granted a big estate in Lucknow.[42] After some time in addition to the family of Shaikh Abdur Rahim, a number of Pathans come and settled and were known as Ram Nagar Pathans.[43] After these Pathans, another group of Shaikhs settled towards the east.[44] They were known as Benehrah Shaikhs. Although these three groups occupied their own areas, the authority of Shaikhzadas was paramount and their power over the neighbourhood was supreme.[45] During the Mughal period most of the subedars of Awadh belonged to these Shaikhzada families.[46] Thus Saadat

Khan had mainly two problems, the increasing power of Rajput chieftains and the ambitions of the Shaikhzadas.

Saadat Khan and Chieftains of Awadh

Saadat Khan led an expedition against the Shaikhzadas of Lucknow in 1722. As mentioned, the Shaikhzadas were locally powerful in Lucknow and they tried to stop Burhan-ul-Mulk's entry into Lucknow.[47] Ultimately Saadat Khan adopted a diplomatic policy. Two stories are known about his entry into Lucknow. First is that he made very slow advance and when he was marching towards Lucknow, halted and encamped at Mahmud Nagar.[48] There, he invited the Shaikhzadas and entertained them with great courtesy and hospitality. These Shaikhzadas accepted the supremacy of Saadat Khan. The second story is that Saadat Khan, passing through Bareilly, reached Farrukhabad where he became a guest of Afghan chief Muhammed Khan Bangash.[49] Muhammed Khan had told Saadat Khan that the Shaikhzadas of Lucknow were troublesome and it was difficult to suppress them, but the other Shaikhs of neighbouring areas of Lucknow had enmity with the Shaikhzadas of Lucknow, so he should take their help.[50] Saadat Khan therefore stopped at Kakori, a few miles west to Lucknow,[51] and made an alliance with the Shaikhs of that place who promised to help the nawab against the Shaikhzadas of Lucknow. Saadat Khan then marched further and camped near Lucknow. The Shaikhzadas of Lucknow tried to resist his army but were defeated and surrendered the Panchmala Palace to the nawab.[52]

Saadat Khan's success enhanced his prestige and subsequently numerous chieftains submitted to him. Saadat Khan accepted their submission and confirmed them in their respective areas and entrusted them with the collection of revenue, provided they paid their dues regularly.[53] Thus Saadat Khan established his authority in the most important part of the suba, Lucknow.

In 1723 Saadat Khan turned his attention to the Rajput chiefs. He found that Raja Mohan Singh Kanhpuria of Tiloi[54] was restive. He had created trouble in the neighbourhood of Tiloi, and plundered the Sayyid of Mustafabad in Salon,[55] then marched against the Bais chief Rana Amar Singh,[56] but two opposing forces were so equally matched that a compromise had to be effected and their boundary was determined after negotiations. Saadat Khan also led expeditions against the Bhale sultans of Jagdishpur, Naihasta Bais of Bachhrawan[57] and made conquests in the south-west of Faizabad region.[58]

It was necessary for Saadat Khan to check the hostile activities of Mohan Singh. He asked Mohan Singh to surrender the paraganas of Faizabad district, and a battle was fought in which Mohan Singh was defeated and killed by the army of the nawab. This created fear among other rebellious zamindars. Consequently many of them paid allegiance to the nawab.[59] On his success Saadat Khan was awarded the title of Burhan-ul-Mulk by Emperor Muhammed Shah (1719–50).[60]

In 1725 Saadat Khan Burhan-ul-Mulk turned his attention towards the northern parganas of the modern districts of Basti and Gorakhpur. In these areas the Banjara[61] people had created a great disturbance. A leader of this community named Tilak Sen of Tilakpur[62] was plundering the districts. He had created an atmosphere of terror which led many people of the region to leave their homes.[63] To punish Tilak Sen, Saadat attacked Gorakhpur. But the army of the nawab could not make any headway against Tilak Sen, because most parts of Gorakhpur were surrounded by forest to which the miscreants fled, only to return on the withdrawal of the nawab's army. This problem of the area continued till the time of Nawab Safdarjang.[64]

In the time of Saadat Khan Baiswara in Unnao district was also facing a political crisis. Its seven parganas of Panhan, Patan, Bihar, Bhagwant Nagar, Magrayar, Ghatampur and Dandikera were ruled by the chiefs of the Bais clan. The Baiswara chiefs had two houses, of Partha Singh and of Harihar Deo. From the former descended the houses of Daundiakhera, Maurawan and Purwa-Ranbirpur, and from the latter sprang the Saibasti and Naibasti.[65] These chiefs had no unity among themselves and were fighting with each other. When Saadat Khan marched to Baiswara all chiefs, except Chet Rai, paid allegiance to him. Chet Rai resisted the nawab in his fort at Pachhimgaon. Saadat Khan was impressed with the bravery of Chet Rai and reduced the payment of the originally assessed revenue by one half.[66]

After Baiswara, Saadat Khan turned to the powerful Rajput Janwar state of Balrampur.[67] Raja Narain Singh, its ruler, had strained relations with the provincial government. Therefore, Saadat attacked him and finally defeated him in battle. Raja Narain Singh submitted and agreed to pay revenue.

After establishing his authority in Janwar state, Saadat Khan led an expedition against Dutta Singh, the Bisen ruler of Gonda. The reason for the attack was that Dutta Singh refused to pay tribute. But in this case the army of Saadat Khan was defeated and his general Alwal Khan was killed. Saadat Khan sent another army against Dutta Singh. This time Dutta Singh accepted the authority of the nawab and agreed to pay tribute.[68]

After establishing his overlordship over almost all the territories of Awadh, Saadat Khan turned his atention to the chiefs of the frontier areas of Awadh. To strengthen the borders he first attacked Mahabat Khan, a hereditary chief of Azamgarh who refused to pay tribute. Hearing of the arrival of the nawab, Mahabat Khan fled to Gorakhpur, but did not feel secure there and returned to Azamgarh. On reaching there he threw himself on the mercy of Saadat Khan who put him into confinement where he died.[69]

In 1729, Saadat Khan led an expedition against Hindu Singh, a Chandel chief, on the western border of the suba.[70] Hindu Singh had built two strong forts, one at Chachendi (Sachendi) and other at Bihnaur, and had organized a strong army. He had also occupied a large territory. With his diplomacy Saadat Khan occupied the fort of Chanchaudi.[71] It helped him extend the western frontier of Awadh up to the vicinity of Kannoj.[72]

In March 1732, Saadat Khan sent his army against Bhagwant Singh, zamindar of Ghazipur and Asothar in the sarkar of Kara Jahanabad, suba Allahabad.[73] The reason was that Bhagwant Singh revolted and created trouble for the faujdar, Jan-Nisar. But Bhagwant defeated the army of the nawab and occupied a considerable portion of Kara Jahanabad. In 1733 Saadat Khan sent another army under Qamruddin to subdue Bhagwant Singh. Although Qamruddin succeeded in expelling Bhagwant Singh from the fort, he could not establish the authority of the nawab in the area permanently. Bhagwant Singh remained unpunished until the end of 1735.[74] However, in 1735 Saadat again attacked, and in the battle Bhagwant Singh was killed and the fort was occupied by the nawab in November 1735.

In 1737 Saadat Khan got news that twenty Rajput chiefs of southern Awadh headed by their leader, Raja Nawal Singh of Tiloi, had made an alliance and committed certain excesses in the southern districts of the provinces.[75] Saadat Khan attacked him. Abul Mansur Khan, commander of the nawab's army, occupied a large part of Tiloi. Meanwhile Abul Mansur learnt that the confederates of the rebellious rajas were concentrating their forces in Amethi. Therefore, he left the reduction of Tiloi and marched against the raja of Amethi. On 12 June 1737, he reached Amethi and defeated the combined Rajput army.

In view of the political condition of Awadh in Saadat Khan's time it seems that different parts of Awadh were under effective control of the influential local zamindars. These chiefs also tried to expand their power and territories. Saadat Khan with ability and military resources compelled them to submission, but they continued their aggression whenever they got a chance. During Saadat Khan's period the territory of Awadh was extended in different directions.

Nawab Abul Mansur Khan Safdarjang (1739–1754)

After the death of Saadat Khan, Abul Mansur Khan Safdarjang, his nephew and son-in-law, became the subedar of Awadh. Safdarjang had been the naib subedar of Awadh from 1724 to 1739.[76] He was familiar with the civil and military affairs of the suba. Safdarjang had fought a number of battles against some of the chiefs of Awadh during Saadat Khan's period. He had, therefore, sufficient practical experience of the power and attitude of the local chiefs of Awadh

When Safdarjang became the governor of Awadh, the main task before him was to check the growing power of the local chiefs. It is evident from the *Tarikh-i-Farah Baksh*[77] that on Saadat Khan's death most of the big chiefs of Awadh broke into the rebellion and tried to regain their freedom in different parts of the suba. Nassarullah and Farhatullah of Amethi Bandagi[78] and the Rajput chiefs of Hasanpur, Tiloi and Garh Amethi, and also the Pathan chiefs of Jagdispur joined hands for widespread insurrection.[79] Safdarjang, acting promptly, attacked the army of rebellious chiefs and defeated them.

Safdarjang's next expedition was against the raja of Tiloi. The raja of Tiloi, who had accepted the supremacy of the Saadat Khan, tried to assert his independence. To suppress his rebellion Safdarjang attacked him on 10 November 1739. The Rajputs were defeated by the nawab's army. However, the raja could not be expelled, he remained in the possession of his estate.[80]

In the beginning of 1741, Safdarjang turned his attention towards Nabinagar[81] and Katesar.[82] He found that the chief was paying tribute and attacked him. The army of the nawab compelled Nawal Singh to vacate the fort on 19 March 1741. Both, the Nawal Singh submitted and his territory was restored to him.[83]

After these local campaigns, Safdarjang was ordered by Emperor Muhammed Shah to help Alivardi Khan against the Marathas in Bengal. In 1748 he fought a war against the Durranis under Ahmed Shah Abdali.[84] While Safdarjang was busy on the military campaign, the administration of the suba was run by Raja Nawal Rai, a deputy governor of Awadh. Safdarjang died in 1754.

Shuja-ud-Daula (1754–1775)

Safdarjang was succeeded by his son Shuja-ud-Daula, after minor opposition.

Shuja-ud-Daula during his whole period as a ruler of Awadh was busy in different campaigns to protect and promote the interests of the Mughal empire. The administration of the suba of Awadh was, therefore, run by his naib. In the beginning of his reign, Ismail Khan Kabuli was appointed as his naib. In 1757 Ismail Khan Kabuli died and Raja Beni Bahadur was appointed as the naib of Awadh.[85]

Shuja-ud-Daula's absence from the actual administration of the suba encouraged different local chiefs to assert their power. For example, during a temporary absence some of the big landlords of the region drove out his revenue collectors (amils).[86]

Taking advantage of the situation, the local chiefs of Awadh not only tried to bacome independent, but also established friendly relations with the enemies of Shuja-ud-Daula, especially the Marathas.

The Bais chiefs were fighting among themselves. Achal Singh, a chief of Baiswara was constantly fighting with the other Bais houses.[87] Raghunath Singh, another chief of Baiswara, declared himself independent. In 1765 after the defeat of Shuja-ud-Daula at Buxar, Rao Raghunath Singh refused to admit the nawab into his fort at Daudia Khera.[88] However, Achal Singh maintained cordial relations with Shuja-ud-Daula and after the defeat of Shuja-ud-Daula at Buxar he was welcomed by Achal Singh at Harha. Shuja-ud-Daula rewarded him by the title of 'raja' and a substantial remission of revenue.[89]

The local chiefs of Awadh throughout Shuja-ud-Daula's period ran the administration of their respective areas independently. Their defiance weakened the suba politically as well as administratively. As already mentioned, the defiant chiefs colluded with external powers; they not only invited the Marathas to attack, but also gave military aid to the English. Raja Balbhadra Singh of Tiloi established good contact with the British. The British sent six regiments to him[90] against Shuja-ud-Daula. According to Donald Butter, in Shuja-ud-Daula's time the whole of province had fallen into disorder and the nawab was financially ruined.[91]

The political history of Awadh from Saadat Khan to Shuja-ud-Daula, shows that there was a continuous tussle for power between local chiefs and the nawabs of Awadh. It is true that these chiefs had neither the resources nor complete unity among themselves to defy the nawab for long,[92] but it is equally true that they never completely surrendered to the nawabs. They rose in rebellion whenever they got a chance. An important reason for chronic rebellions was the frequent absence of the nawabs of Awadh from the suba. Whenever the Mughal emperor faced any uprising in any part of the empire often the nawab had to go to his help. For example, Saadat Khan fought against Nadir Shah, and Safdarjang and Shuja-ud-Daula waged continuous battle against the Marathas. In such a situation it was difficult for the nawabs to pay continuous attention to the law and order position of the suba effectively. The collection of revenue from the zamindars mainly depended on local chiefs. Consequently the tussle between the nawab and them allowed the zamindars and others to gain more and more power. This affected the socio-economic and even the political life of the suba adversely. It was against this background that one finds the emergence of *madad-i-maash* holders as an important class socially as well as politically.

THE STATE AND REVENUE FREE GRANTS

The assignment of revenue free land grants originated in ancient times. Such grants were given to men engaged in religious persuits, Brahmans, and also to religious institutions. References to such grants are available from the first century AD.[93] However, from the fourth century the significance of such grants increased.[94] From the Gupta period[95] onwards revenue free lands grants were made on large scale. In Harsha's time[96] these were on an even large scale: Harsha granted one hundred villages of one thousand ploughs to individual Brahmans.[97] Another reference shows that the Pallavas of the south granted a number of revenue free assignments to temples.[98]

In ancient India revenue free grants were know as *brahmadeyas*,[99] *agraharas*[100] and *devadanas*.[101] Since Brahmans were understood as men of pious caste and according to the varna system they alone were allowed to accept donations, they had a monopoly on such assignment of revenue free land.

It seems that the main objective behind these assignment of revenue free grant was to patronize Brahmans, the most influential caste. All important rituals were performed by them. Being members of the highest caste they could mobilise society according to their own will. The social influence of Brahmans in society also gave them considerable political importance. The ancient Indian state found it easiest to get social support by partronizing the Brahmans through the assignment of land grants.

In ancient India the size of revenue free grants was big. In most cases land donations given to temples and Brahmans were made in terms of whole villages. It may be mentioned that large grant holdings helped the grantees in the expansion of their own property. They needed a large number of people to work on their lands. Consequently, it gave rise of a kind of feudal relation leading to the exploitation of the peasantry.[102] In principle, the grantees were not allowed to sell, mortgage or alienate the landed property thus bestowed. However, references have been found to temple authorities transferring and selling *devadana* land frequently.[103]

In the thirteenth century when the Turks came to the power, they continued with land grants and other types of subsistence allowances to the needy, the learned, persons of noble lineage and religious institutions. Since the *mashaikh*[104] and *ulema*[105] commanded great respect amongst the people, it was in the interest of ruling classes to gain their goodwill. The elite sought their blessings the state in turn gave financial support in terms of money and land grants to them. The land grant conferred upon them for subsistence became fairly important from the social, economic and religious points of view.[106]

In the early period of Delhi sultanate the terms used for subsistence allowance were *milk*,[107] *wazifa*,[108] *inam*[109] and *augaf*.[110] Subsequently they were also known as *wajh-i-maash* and *wajh-i-milk*, and became popular and were used as such in the official documents for all revenue free land grants conferred upon the scholars and other religious institutions.[111]

Regarding revenue free land grants Zia-ud-Din Barani says that a large portion of the revenue in the territories annexed by the sultans was alienated as *milk*, *inam*, *idrarat*[112] and *waqf* endowments.[113] This indicates that the state during the sultanate period extended considerable support to the needy, to scholars and to persons of religious background. Land grants were small areas of entire villages,[114] the size depending on the status and functions of the grantee. However, these grants were assigned in the cultivated and uncultivated but cultivable areas.[115]

During the Mughal period certain changes were made in the terminology and nature of such grants. Under the Mughals the term *madad-i-maash* grant was more commonly used for revenue free land grant as compared with *milk*, *wajh-i-maash* and *inam*. However, another term, *sayurghal*, was also used in the documents of Akbar's reign in particular. There is a separate chapter in the *Ain-i-Akbari* entitled *sayurghal*.[116] The term *sayurghal* is of Central Asian origin,[117] and was not in common usage in the Mughal period. Indeed, one farman of Babur (1526–30) regarding revenue free land grants bears the word *sayurghal*.[118] But in another two farmans of the same period the term *madad-i-maash* has been used.[119] The documents from Akbar's reign onwards that portain to grants generally bear the word *madad-i-maash*.

As synonyms of *madad-i-maash* the terms *aimma*,[120] *inam*[121] and *milk* have been also used in Mughal documents. Nonetheless all these terms, *madad-i-maash*, *sayurghal*, *milk*, *inam* and *aimma*, were used for revenue free grants.

According to Abul Fazl, two types of subsistence allowance were given to grantees, allowances in cash, known as *wazifa*, and assigned lands known as *milk* or *madad-i-maash* grants.[122] Some modern scholars are of the opinion that there was a difference between *sayurghal* and *madad-i-maash* grants.[123] However, *sayurghal* and *madad-i-maash* terms in Mughal documents seem to be synomyms. Shireen Moosvi has clearly explained that both *sayurghal* and *madad-i-maash* were granted in terms of land. According to her, 'Abul Fazl has used the term quite loosely, making it at a time synonym of *madad-i-maash* when he says, *sayurghal* of *Afghan* Chaudharies were converted into *khalisa* or when he speaks *zamin-i-sayurghal*.' It seems that initially the Mughals used the term *sayurghal* for grants, but as they consolidated their empire they preferred to use the commonly understood term *madad-i-maash* instead of *sayurghal*.[125]

NOTES

1. Abul Fazl says, 'The name of Awadh is derived from Ajoydya. Rama Chandra, seventh Avtar of Hinduism, was born in Ajoydhya'. *Ain-i-Akbari* (hereafter *Ain.*), vol. II, English translation by H.S. Jarret and Sir J.N. Sarkar, Delhi 1978, p. 182. Richard Barnett, *North India Between Empires, Awadh, the Mughals and British, 1720–1801*, London, 1980, p. 19.
2. A.B.M. Habibullah, *Foundation of Muslim Rule in India*, Allahabad, 1961, p. 9.
3. *Ain.*, vol. II (English trans.), p. 182.

4. Ibid., p. 181.
5. Ibid.
6. Ibid.
7. Irfan Habib, *An Atlas of Mughal Empire*, Delhi, 1982, p. 30.
8. H.R. Nevill, *Bahraich District Gazetteer*, Lucknow, 1921, p. 6.
9. H.C. Irwine, *The Garden of India*, vol. I, Lucknow, 1973, pp. 16–17.
10. Irfan Habib, op. cit.
11. H.C. Irwine, op. cit. vol. 1, p. 17.
12. Ibid.
13. Donald Butter, *Topography and Statistics of Southern Districts of Awadh*, edited by Safi Ahmed, Delhi, 1982, p. 25.
14. Ibid.
15. Ibid.
16. Ibid.
17. Leather Bag and a rope was used to raise the water when the river bank was on a sufficient height. The rope being passed over, either a rude weighty pully made a thick block of wood a foot in diameter or win a slight, rickety, irregular cylinder of split bamboos. Donald Butter, *Topography*, p. 46.
18. The basket was used when the bank of river was perpendicular and close to the water. The basket is pulled by two men, each of whom commands the swing of basket by a rope and held in each hand and attached to the basket which woven of split bamboos. Donald Butter, p. 67.
19. *Dugla* was used when the bank of river was a round shape. The water was lifted by four men who took the work by turns and raised the water 6 feet. By this means 3 *bighas* of land could be irrigated in a day. Ibid.
20. At some places where the bank of the river was cut into very neat zigzag channels, water was raised by a series of baskets and different height. Ibid.
21. Irfan Habib, *Agrarian System of Mughal India*, Bombay, 1963, p. 29.
22. *Dhenkali* was used where a well was closed to the surface. It was simplest method of irrigation from the wells. Irfan Habib and Tapan Ray Chaudhuri, *The Cambridge Economic History of India*, vol. I, Cambridge, 1982, p. 211.
23. *Charas* was used into the wells of great depth. When the quantity of water was more it could be drawn by one man having a small leathorn or iron bucket at each end of a rope. Donald Butter, *Topography*, p. 67.
24. Ibid., p. 68.
25. Ibid.
26. Ibid.
27. H.R. Nevill, *Faizabad District Gazetteer*, Allahabad, 1921, p. 33.
28. *Ain.*, vol. II (English trans.), p. 182.
29. H.C. Irwin, *Garden of India*, vol. I, p. 16.
30. Elizabeth Whitcombe, *Agrarian Condition in Northern India, 1860–1900*, Delhi, 1971, p. 23.
31. Regarding the crops of the suba during spring season Abul Fazl has mentioned the names such as wheat, Kabuli gram (*nakhud-i-kabuli*), Indian gram (*nakhud-*

i-Hind), barley, pot harbs, pappy, safflower, lineseed, mustard oil, adas, arzan, peas, persian muskmelons, Indian muskmelons, kur rice, *ajwain*, onions, fennugaek and carrots. *Ain.*, vol. II (English trans.), p. 82. Also see, W.H. Moreland, *India at the Death of Akbar*, Delhi, 1974, p. 303.

32. Abul Fazl has mentioned the following *kharif* crops sown in the suba: sugar cane (*paunda*), common rice, dark-coloured rice manji rice, pot herbs, sesame seed, *moth, maash, mung, jowar, lahdrah, bajra, lobia, kodaran, kari* (lowest grade) millets, *shamakh*, gal, arzan, mandawa, indigo, hemp, *turya*, turmeric, *kachalu, kult, watermelon, pan, singhara* (water nut) and arhar. *Ain.*, vol. II (English trans.), pp. 82–4. Also see Moreland, *India at the Death of Akbar*, p. 303.
33. The measured areas of the suba were 1,01,71,181 *bighas. Ain.*, vol. II (English trans.), p. 184. Also see, Sir J.N. Sarkar, *India of Aurangzeb*, Calcutta, 1901, pp. 37–8.
34. Abul Fazl has mentioned the names of paraganas or mahals of the sarkar of Awadh as Awadh ba Haveli, Ambodha, Ibrahimabad, Anheona, Pachhimrath, Bilhari, Basodhi, Thana-Bhadam, Baktha, Dayabad, Rudauli, Silak, Sultanpur, Satanpur, Subcha, Sarwapath, Satrikh, Gawarchak Kishni, Mangalso, Nainpur, *Ain.*, vol. II (English trans.), pp. 184–5.
35. According to Abul Fazl, the sarkar of Gorakhpur comprised the parganas of Utraula, Unhaula, Binakpur, Baubhanparah, Bawalparah, Telpur, Cheluparah, Daryaparah, Dewaparah, Kotlah, Rihli, Rasulpur, Ghosi, Ramgrah, Gauri, Gorakpur ba Haveli, two mahals, Katihala, Rahlaparah, Mahauli, Mandawah, Mandalh, Maghar and Ratanpur. *Ain.*, vol. II (English trans.), p. 186.
36. Sarkar Bahraich comprised the parganas such as Bahraich ba Haveli, Barah, Husampur, Dangun, Rajhat, Sujhauli, Sultanpur, Kakhrpur, Firozabad, Nawahgarh, Kharonsa. *Ain.*, vol. II (English trans.), p. 187.
37. Sarkar of Kairabad had the following parganas: Barror Anjarah, Baswah, Pali, Baswan, Basrah, Bhurwarah, Basara, Piha, Chhatyapur, Khairabad two mahals, Sandi, Sarah, Sadrpur, Gopaman, Kheri, Khairigarh, Kharkhela, Khankatman, Laharpur, Machharhatta, Nimkhar, Hargaraon, *Ain.*, vol. II (English trans.), pp. 184–8.
38. The sarkar of Lucknow comprised the parganas of Amethi, Unam (Unnao), Isauli, Asiyun, Asoha, Unchagaon, Bilgram, Bangarman, Bijnaur, Bari, Bahriman, Pangwan, Betholi, Panhan, Parsandan, Patan, Barashkor, Jahalotar, Dewi, Deorakh, Dadrah, Raubarpur, Ramkot, Sandilah, Saidpur, Sarosi, Satanpur, Sahali, Sidhaur, Sidhpur, Sandi, Saron, Fatehpur, Garh, Amethi, Kursi, Kakori, Kangrah, Ghatampur, Kachhaupur, Goranda, Khumbi, Lucknow ba Haveli, Lashkar, Malihabad, Mallawan, Mohan, Moraon, Madian, Mohanah, Manawi, Makraed, Harha, Hardoi, Hanbar. *Ain.*, vol. II (English trans.), pp. 188–90.
39. Richard B. Barnett, *North India Between Empires, Awadh, the Mughals and the British, 1720–1801*, London, 1908. During the end of Akbar's reign Jawahar Khan was subedar. In Shahjahan's reign the subedar of suba was Sultan Ali Shah Qali Khan. Abdul Halim Sharar, *Lucknow: The last Phase of an Orient Culture*, London, 1975, pp. 38–9.

40. For the early life and career of Saadat Khan, see A.L. Srivastava, *First Two Nawabs of Awadh*, Agra, 1954.
41. Srivastava, *First Two Nawabs*, p. 31.
42. Sharar, *Lucknow: The Last Phase of an Oriental Culture*, p. 37.
43. Ibid., p. 37. Ramnagar was a town in the present district of Bareilly.
44. Ibid.
45. Ibid., p. 38.
46. Sharar, *Lucknow: The Last Phase*, p. 38.
47. Ibid., p. 41.
48. Ibid.
49. Srivastava, *First Two Nawabs*, p. 32.
50. Sharar, *Lucknow: The Last Phase*, p. 42.
51. Srivastava, *First Two Nawabs*, p. 33.
52. Ibid.
53. Ibid.
54. Tiloi is a village in Pargana Mohanganj, tahsil Mohaaj Ganj, district Rae Bareli. *District Gazetteer of Rae Bareli* by H.R. Nevill, Lucknow, 1923, p. 230. It is about 18 miles north-east of Rae Bareli. Srivastava, *First Two Nawabs*, p. 34.
55. H.R. Nevill, *District Gazetteer of Rae Bareli*, pp. 82–3.
56. Rana Amar Singh was head of Saibansi clan Khajurgaon estate. Srivastava, *First Two Nawabs*, p. 34.
57. Bachhrawan is 19 miles north-west of Rae Bareli, Srivastava, *First Two Nawabs*, p. 34.
58. H.R. Nevill, *District Gazetteer of Rae Bareli*, p. 83.
59. Srivastava, *First Two Nawabs*, p. 35.
60. Ibid.
61. A community of merchant robbers. Ibid., p. 39.
62. Tilakpur was in Gorakhpur.
63. *Gorakhpur District Gazetteer*, Allahabad, 1909, p. 182.
64. *Basti District Gazetteer*, Allahabad, 1907, p. 153.
65. Srivastava, *First Two Nawabs*, p. 40.
66. H.R. Nevill, *District Gazetteer of Unnao*, Allahabad, 1934, p. 123.
67. Balrampur, in the modern district of Gonda, was fast rising to importance during the early eighteenth century. The original ancestors of Janwar chiefs belonged to Gujrat. Some time in fourteenth century they migrated to Awadh and founded the great Ikauna State. One of their descendants in the seventh generation from the original immigrants separated from the main branch and occupied the tract between the Kapti and Kuwana. Balram Das, one of the descendants of this dynasty, founded the town of Balrampur. Srivastava, *First Two Nawabs*, p. 40.
68. Srivastava, *First Two Nawabs*, p. 41.
69. Ibid., p. 43.
70. Ibid.
71. Ibid., pp. 43–4.

72. Ibid., p. 44.
73. Ibid., pp. 44–5.
74. Ibid., p. 47.
75. Ibid., p. 57.
76. Ibid., p. 87.
77. *Tarikh-i-Farah Baksh* is written by Muhammed Faiz Bakhsh. It has been translated by W. Hoey under the title of *Memoirs of Delhi and Faizabad*, Allahabad, 1889.
78. Amethi Bandagi is 14 miles south-west of Lucknow, Srivastava, *First Two Nawabs*, p. 91.
79. Srivastava, *First Two Nawabs*, p. 91.
80. Ibid., p. 92.
81. Nabinagar is 20 miles north-east of Sitapur and 3 miles north-west of Laharpur. H.R. Nevill, *District Gazetteer of Sitapur*, 1923, p. 161.
82. Katesar is at a distance of 2 miles south of Sitapur. Ibid., p. 196.
83. Srivastava, *First Two Nawabs*, p. 93.
84. H.C. Irwine, *Garden of India*, vol. 1, p. 69.
85. Richard B. Barnett, *North India Between Empires*, p. 55.
86. Srivastava, *Shuja-ud-Daula (1754–65)*, vol. I, Agra, 1961, p. 46.
87. H.R. Nevill, *District Gazetteer of Unnao*, pp. 126–7.
88. Ibid., p. 127.
89. Ibid.
90. Ibid.
91. Donald Butter, *Topography*, p. 109.
92. Ibid.
93. Romila Thapar, 'Social Mobility in Ancient India', in R.S. Sharma and D.N. Jha (eds.), *Indian Society: Historical Probings*, Delhi, 1974, p. 113.
94. Ibid.
95. Fourth century AD. to sixth century AD.
96. AD 606 to 647.
97. D. Devahuti, *Harsha: A Political Study*, Oxford, 1970, pp. 168–9.
98. 117 Pallava documents show that nearly 53 record donations made to the temples. Out of these 53 a dozen or more inscriptions refer to the gift of a plot of land and whole villages. D.N. Jha, 'Temples as Landed Magnets in Early Medieval South India', *Indian Society*, p. 202.
99. A *brahmadeya* was given to the Brahmans, R.S. Sharma, *Aspects of Political Ideas and Institutions in Ancient India*, Delhi, 1968, pp. 255–6.
100. An *agrahara* was assigned to the Brahmans and religious institutions. Ibid., pp. 321–2.
101. The *devadana* was granted to temples. D.N. Jha, 'Temples as Landed Magnets', *Indian Society*, p. 202.
102. Ibid., p. 212.
103. Ibid., p. 208.
104. Persons of noble lineage.

105. People of the priest class.
106. I.H. Siddiqui, 'Wajh-i-Maash Grants Under the Afghan Kings (1451–1555)', in K.A. Nizami (ed.), *Medieval India: A Miscellany*, vol. II, Bombay, 1972, p. 18.
107. Revenue free land grants.
108. Subsistence allowance in cash.
109. Revenue land grants. According to Zia-ud-din Barani (*Tarikh-i-Firozshahi*) the land grant given to the needy was called *inam*. Elliot and Dowson, *History of India*, vol. III, p. 118.
110. *Auqaf* is plural of *waqf*. The land grants made for the maintenance of a religious shrines was called *waqf* or *auqaf*. I.H. Siddiqui, 'Wajh-i-Maash', *Medieval India: A Miscellany*, vol. II, p. 18.
111. The earliest reference to the *wajh-i-maash* grant is found in the official document of Firozshah's reign. Ibid., p. 18.
112. Pensions.
113. R.P. Tripathi, *Some Aspects of Muslim Administration*, Allahabad, 1964, p. 255.
114. There are number of reference which indicate that during the Lodi period (1451–1525) the *wajh-i-maash* holders occupied a sizeable area of land grants under their control. I.H. Siddiqui, 'Wajh-i-Maash': *A Miscellany*, vol. II, pp. 22–3.
115. Ibid., pp. 21–2.
116. Abul Fazl, *Ain-i-Akbari*, vol. I, English translation by H. Blochmann, Delhi, 1977, pp. 278–85.
117. In medieval Iran generally the term *sayurghal* was used for revenue free land grants. Roger Savory, a modern scholar of Iranian History mentions that during the Safavid period religious persons were granted beneficiaries and immunities from taxation of the types known as *sayurghal*. *Iran Under the Safavids*, Cambridge, 1980, p. 186.
118. Moinuddin Momin, 'A *Sayurghal* of Babur', Proceedings of the Indian Historical Records Commission, 1961, pt. II, pp. 49–52.
119. Irfan Habib, *Agrarian System*, p. 298.
120. J.S. Grewal and B.N. Goswamy, *The Mughals and Jogis of Jakhbar*, Simla, 1967, p. 46.
121. Ibid., p. 51. The term *inam* was used in medieval south India more commonly than medieval north India. Richard Maxwell Eaton, *Sufis of Bijapur (1300–1700)*, New Jersey, 1978, pp. 205–42.
122. *Ain.*, vol. I (English trans.), p. 278.
123. Moreland writes that the *sayurghal* was an allowance paid in cash or granted in land. *Agrarian System of Muslim India*, Delhi, 1968, p. 277. N.A. Siddiqui, observes that the subsistence allowance in land was known as *madad-i-maash*. The two types of grant were covered by the general term *sayurghal*. *Land Revenue Administration Under the Mughals (1700–1750)*, Bombay, 1970, p. 123.
124. Shireen Moosvi, '*Sayurghal* Statistics in the *Ain-i-Akbari*', *Indian Historical Review*, 1976, vol. II, no. 2, p. 28.

125. This hypothesis can be examined from the fact that the word *sayurghal* was hardly ever used in seventeenth century in grant documents. Irfan Habib, *Agrarian System*, p. 298. In the suba of Awadh, except for a few documents, *madad-i-maash* term has been used on the bulk of the documents of land grants of the seventeenth and eighteenth centuries.

CHAPTER 2

Madad-i-Maash Grants: Policy and Assignments

The assignment of *madad-i-maash* grants to the needy and pious and to intellectual persons was a religious requirement of the state under Islamic law. Under the Mughals this practice received greater attention of and the Mughal rulers streamlined the system, making it more effective. Emperor Akbar took keen interest in the system of assignments as is evident from the fact that in the *Ain-i-Akbari*, pargana wise assignment of these grants are recorded.[1]

Akbar specified the procedure of these assignments to prevent their misuse and to keep an effective watch over them.[2] According to Abul Fazl, people of four classes were eligible for such grants: the learned,[3] saints,[4] the poor[5] and men of noble lineage.[6] It may be mentioned that this categorization applied to men of all religions.

Besides determining eligibility for such grants, Akbar made many other changes. He ordered the cancellation of *madad-i-maash* grants of the Afghans. This order was issued with the idea to break the monopoly of Afghans over large areas.[7] During Akbar's reign Afghans had started anti-Mughal activities, revolting against the Mughals and always trying to regain their political authority. They were not reconciled to the establishment of Mughal rule. It seems, therefore, that Akbar was to break the political hold of the Afghans at the local level by confiscating their grants.[8]

Akbar ordered the consolidation of the scattered holdings of *madad-i-maash* grants.[9] This was considered favourable for both the government and the grantees.[10] It seems that the main objectives behind this order were: to make the administration of *madad-i-maash* grants more efficient so that the state could keep a check on the activities of the grantees, to facilitate development of the land on large scale (it is established fact that consolidated land holdings are more beneficial to the cultivator as compared to the scattered holdings), and to encourage the grantees to engage in agriculture effectively. The position of *madad-*

i-maash holders changed from mere parasite class to active participants in the rural development of the region. This considerably improved the economic life of the grantees as well as tenants working under them.[11]

Akbar tried to keep the grantees at the place of their original grant because it seems that some grantees used to acquire new grants at more fertile places, leaving the places of their original grants. This must have created some administrative problems.[12] Akbar ordered that everyone who left his original place of grant had to surrender one-fourth of his land to receive a new grant.[13]

It may be noted that these reforms aimed at enhancing administrative efficiency but were not successful. It was reported that corruption continued in the assignment of *madad-i-maash* grants and people obtained large areas of land which they did not deserve.[14] Therefore, a new order was passed, according to which all grantees were required to appear before the emperor personally with their documents if they wanted to continue with their grants.[15] In case they did not follow the orders their grants were to be confiscated.[16] But this was not implemented effectively. On enquiry it was found that the grantees indulged in malpractices and cheated the government officials either by misrepresenting their condition or forging the documents of the grant.[17]

Akbar issued another regulation to stop forgery. All grants exceeding 100 *bighas*, if left unspecified in the farman, were to be reduced by two-fifths and the remaining three-fifths were to be converted into *khalsa* (crown lands[18]). However, this rule was not applied to Irani and Turani women grantees.[19] But when Akbar came to know that those women grantees were also involved in fraudulent activities, he passed an order to enquire whether they also held grants exceeding 100 *bighas*. It was also to be ascertained whether they had acuqired their grants lawfully or otherwise.[20]

In spite of these regulations, the fraud could not be stopped completely. It was found that holders of such grants were guilty of indulging in illegal practices. The emperor ordered that Mir Sadr-i-Jahan bring such grantees before him. It was decided that the *sadr* with the concurrence of Abul Fazl should increase or decrease the *madad-i-maash* grants after examining the merit of the cases.

Regarding the quality of lands of *madad-i-maash* grants, Akbar issued an order that all grants should be assigned in the cultivated and waste cultivable land.[21] If the whole grant consisted of cultivated land, one-fourth of it should be resumed, and a fresh document for the remaining land was to be issued to the grantee.[22]

Finally, and the most significant reform in the institution of *madad-i-maash* grant made by Akbar, was the check on the power of officials managing such grants. Akbar discovered that the *qazis*[23] were in the habit of taking bribes from grant holders.[24] Consequently the emperor passed an order to dismiss all corrupt *qazis*.[25] Akbar also tried to check the power of *sadr-us-sudur*.[26] He found that the *sadr* was bribed by grantees to protect their interests.[27] To stop such practices Akbar adopted the policy of replacing the *sadrs* after short duration.[28]

All such reforms were intended to keep the grantees under control. Since they were a strong social group at the local level, Akbar tried to make them realize that their anti-government activity was to their detriment. Their privileges would remain so long as they remained loyal to the State. This is illustrated from the steps that Akbar took to augment the strength of the Indian Muslim (Shaikhzadas) *madad-i-maash* holders in the Mughal nobility. According to a recent study, Akbar recruited some Indian Muslim *madad-i-maash* holders into Mughal nobility.[29] Such favours were motivated by the idea to create a class of loyalists at local level to check and counter the anti-royal elements. Besides, Akbar imposed a check on the power of the officials who were incharge also, so that a genuine and loyal *madad-i-maash* holder should not be harassed.

Jahangir continued the policy of Akbar. In his memoir, he mentions that he confirmed all the land grants assigned by his father.[30] In fact, he assigned *madad-i-maash* grants more liberally than Akbar. Jahangir writes, 'By a stroke of the pen I confirmed the subsistence lands of the *aimas* (charity lands) with in the dominions. . . . I gave order to Miran Sadar-i-Jahan . . . that he should present everyday deserving people (worthy of charity).'[31]

In the ninth year of his reign (1613–14) Jahangir assigned several *madad-i-maash* grants to the poor and also distributed a large sum of money among them.[32] In 1619 he granted 44,780 *bighas*, two entire villages and 320 *kharwar* (ass loads) of grain in Kashmir.[33] These references could be multiplied. Thus one would find that during Jahangir's reign *madad-i-maash* grants were assigned on a large scale. He called the *madad-i-maash* grantees the *lashkar-i-duagon* or army of prayers.[34] According to him this army of prayers was as important for the betterment of the empire as the real army.[35]

To make the grantees loyal to the state, Jahangir imposed some restrictions. He ordered that all such grants were to be made by him in person.[36] Therefore grantees should appear before him in person for the renewal and confirmation of their grants. Those who did not were liable to be punished by confiscation of their grants. For example, in 1623 Jahangir confiscated 20,289 *bighas* of land assigned by Akbar to the *mujawirs*[37] of Ajmer. The resumption was made because some of the *mujawirs* did not appear personally before the emperor.[38] In his early years of his reign, Jahangir resumed the *madad-i-maash* grants of 3,207 *bighas*, 2,727 *bighas*, 1,714 *bighas* and 14 *biswas* of the Sayyid *math* because the original grantees were dead, and perhaps non-represented them personally at the court.[39] There were many other grantees whose grants were resumed as they failed to appear personally before the emperor.[40]

Besides confirmation and resumption of *madad-i-maash* grants, Jahangir also reduced and increased the holdings according to the performance of the grantees. A document of Jahangir's reign indicates that Musammat Bega Khanam, the wife of Rahman Beg, possessed a land grant of 60 *bighas* in the village Dhankti, sarkar Hajipur, suba Bihar. After her death, half the grant was revoked and the remainder renewed in favour of her heirs.[41] There are some other references regarding the reduction of the size of the *madad-i-maash* grants.[42] It seems that during Jahangir's reign the practice started was that of reduction of the sizes of grants. About half the area could be claimed back at the time of renewal.

The question arises when Jahangir was liberal in assignment of *madad-i-maash* grants, why was the practice of reclaiming half or near half of the original grant was practised even if the assignee continued to be loyal to the State. There appear to be two probable reasons. First, the idea was to assign the *madad-i-maash* grants in cultivated and cultivable land. Over a period of time when cultivable land turned into cultivated land, yields, must have exceeded what was expected from the assigned land, therefore, the State would have thought to resume some portion of the grant, without materially affecting the actual yield enjoyed by the grantee. This is confirmed by the fact that the distinction between cultivated and cultivable land is mentioned in the original assignment orders, but in cases of renewal the world 'cultivable' is often missing.

Second, through the practice of assigning cultivated and cultivable land in original assignment, and then resumption of some cultivated land at the time of renewal, helped in expanding the cultivated area, making cultivated land available for assignment in *madad-i-maash* grants along with uncultivated lands to others. This must have provided a mechanism for bringing more and more land under the plough.

The needs of *madad-i-maash* holders were also important considerations for the state. In cases where the members of the family of *madad-i-maash* holder increased, the size of *madad-i-maash* grant originally assigned to the grantee was also increased.[43] It may be mentioned that the available references to the increase of *madad-i-maash* grant lands indicate that when the size of an allotment was increased, a new document was issued to the grantee, which bore the names of some co-sharer *madad-i-maash* holders in addition to the names mentioned in earlier documents.[44] Thus, during Jahangir's reign, *madad-i-maash* grants were given liberally, but by adopting the regulations of renewal, reductions and resumptions to keep a check on the power and need of the grantees.

During Shahjahan's reign a number of changes were made in the assignment of *madad-i-maash* grants. He categorized the recipients of the grants. According to Yusuf Mirak, author of *Mazhar-i-Shahjahani* people of three classes were eligible to receive them,[45] officials (who received grant in lieu of salaries), scholars and memorisers of the Koran, and Sayyids, Shaikhs and Mughals by descent who eschewing the urge for the greater gain, retired to a corner and were content with a little *madad-i-maash* grant from the court and had no other means of livelihood.

Apart from these three classes of *madad-i-maash* holders there was a fourth, consisting of zamindars who were also *arbabs* (*chaudharis*) and *muqadamms*.[46] It may be significant that the assignment of *madad-i-maash* grants to zamindars was introduced by Shahjahan. Although the *Mazhar-i-Shahjahani* states that under the regime of Nurjahan zamindars purchased *madad-i-maash* grants,[47] hardly any document is available about the assignment of *madad-i-maash* grant to the zamindars by the State.

However, the change in Shahjahan's reign created problems for the grantees of other classes. As is well known, zamindars were most influential class of rural society and could use their influence to obtain *madad-i-maash* grants illegally.

In this connection Irfan Habib writes, 'It depricates this practice by making use of their authority these local officials got the best lands and compelled the peasants to cultivate them without making any effort themselves.'[48]

Moreover, such *madad-i-maash* grants must have increased the economic power of the zamindars. On the one hand, zamindars were entitled to collect land revenue and got *nankar*[49] in lieu of such service to the state; they also received *malikana*[50] rights for their *zamindari* lands. Over and above this zamindars now got *madad-i-maash* lands revenue free, and could utilize the income from then to strengthen their power and become a threat to the state.

Reference is also found to Shahjahan assigning *madad-i-maash* to his military men. According to Abdul Hamid Lahori, author of the *Badshahnama*, Shahjahan while desposing his general Alivardi Khan in 1644, gave him *madad-i-maash* grant lands yielding 34,00,000 *dams* (Rs. 8,500) annually.[51] However, such references are rare. The bulk of the grants were given to the needy, scholars, and persons of noble birth who had no source of their livelihood.

Shahjahan made the administration of *madad-i-maash* grants more effective than earlier. He took stern action against the irregularities which prevailed in the office of *sadr-us-sudur*. He dismissed Musavi Khan, the *sadr-us-sudur*, from his office on the complaints of Jalal.[52]

To check the forgery, Shahjahan enforced the following regulations:[53]

1. The revenue of one crop (*fasl*) of all *madad-i-maash* lands whether in *khalsa* or in *jagirs*[54] of the nobles was to withheld and deposited elsewhere.
2. The withheld revenue was to be given to the holders of grants when their certificates (*asnad*) were verified and their claims established.
3. Holders of grants personally known to the emperor were exempt from those orders.
4. The grantees residing in the capitals of the provinces were to contact the governors regarding their problems.

These regulations could not however be implemented, becuase they led to great resentment among the grant holders. There was every possiblity of harassment of the grant holders at the hands of the official concern. These regulations not only enhanced the power of these officials, but were likely to empower them to collect illegal dues at the time of the enquiry of the validity of the documents.

To avoid such a situation, Shahjahan passed other regulations:

1. The withheld revenue was to be paid to the grantee and the rent of next crop to be withheld if necessary verification was not obtained.[55]
2. The grantees residing in the capital and suburbs were to get their

grants verified by the chief *sadr*. Those who held land through a royal farman of Akbar, duly confirmed during Jahangir's reign and renewed by Shahjahan, were allowed to retain their grants. The latter were to be verified by the local *sadr* after consultation with the governor.[56]

3. The *madad-i-maash* grants of soldiers and artisans were to be resumed.[57]
4. The grants of deceased assignees were to be renewed to their rightful heirs. To examine the genuine claim of the heir of the deceased grantee it was decided that the document should bear the term *ma farzandan* (with sons), otherwise the grant in question was to be included in *khalsa*, and if its possessors were considered deserving, a separate report was sought regarding them.[58]

There are several examples which indicate that in the light of the reports during the reign of Shahjahan, several *madad-i-maash* grants were either restored or revoked.[59] However, a large number of *madad-i-maash* grant documents of Shahjahan's reign show that the Mughal administration adopted a generous attitude and restored the entire land grants to the heirs of many original grantees.[60] For example, Shahjahan confirmed the whole grant of 200 *bighas* to the Jogisthan Nath and Bhau Nath in the village Narot, suba of Lahore.[61] He showed even greater generosity in the case of the *mujawirs* of Ajmer by allowing them a general exemption in inheritance of the *madad-i-maash* grants.[62]

In 1634 Shahjahan passed an order about resumption of the grant of undeserving grantees, but had to withdraw it because his favourite daughter Jahanara was seriously burnt and Shahjahan thought she suffered owing to harassment by some grantees. He abolished this regulation.[63] It is important to note that such happenings indicate that *madad-i-maash* holders were not only understood to be a pious class among the masses, but the state had also the same feeling regarding the religious merit of the grantees. On the whole Shahjahan's liberal policy helped the grantees to obtain economic backing from the state. By the time of Aurangzeb, *madad-i-maash* holders emerged an economically and socially important class.

Aurangzeb continued a generous policy towards the *madad-i-maash* holders. The area assigned in grant considerably increased under him. A number of references indicate that in the suba of Awadh many grantees possessed one 100 *bighas* or more as *madad-i-maash* grant.

Under Aurangzeb's reign, normally the grant was renewed without reduction in the size of the holding.[64] In 1664 Shaikh Shukurullah had the whole grant of 200 *bighas* renewed in pargana Sailak, sarkar Lucknow.[65] In 1665 Sayyid Taj Muhammad was got his whole grant of 25 *bighas* renewed in pargana Sailak, sarkar Lucknow.[66] There are many other references which indicate that grants were renewed without reduction.[67]

However, there are a few contrary cases. A document indicates that during Aurangzeb's reign Sayyid Habib held a grant of 200 *bighas* in pargana Bhagalpur, sarkar Monghyr, suba Bihar. After his death only half the grant was renewed to his heirs.[68] In the absence of specific reasons in cases where the size of *madad-i-maash* grant was reduced at the time of renewal, it could only be assumed that this was done due to local conditions. Local officials must have used their discretion in recommending cases of renewal and in the light of the complaints received from the grantees against the high-handedness of local officials, consequently, Aurangzeb had to issue a farman in 1690 stating the all *madad-i-maash* grantees had hereditary rights.[69]

Aurangzeb's farman of 1690 decalred that the land of grantees, *aima-i-uzzam*, 'confirmed by valid farman old and new would be retained completely and fully without loss or reduction by the heirs of deceased grantees generation after generation'.[70] This farman also specified the terms and conditions of the renewal of *madad-i-maash* grants to the heirs. Further, it insisted that since the *madad-i-maash* grant was loan (*ariyat*) and not property, its inheritance was to be governed by imperial order, not by *shariat*. Thus it allowed a direct share to the grantee if his father had died; it deprived a daughter of her share if she was married. It was laid down that a widow might keep her husband's grant for life before it passed to her husband's heirs.[71] If the husband had no heirs, the grant would be assigned to the relatives of the widow. If a grantee died leaving behind his daughter as heir and othagnatic heirs (*asbat*) also, in *madad-i-maash* grants yet to be whole assigned to the daughter. If a grantee left his mother, grandmother and other ladies whose maintenance was to be made by him according to the Koran (*Sahib-i-Farza*), the land was divided among them according to the Islamic code (*Mulabi-i-share-i-sharif*). If a grantee left a nephew or cousin as heir, his land was to be granted according to prescribed rules in *shariat*. If a man died without leaving behind him any heirs, his *madad-i-maash* grant was to be resumed and as imperial property (*bait-ul-mal*)[72]

This farman not only accepted the hereditary rights of *madad-i-*

maash holders but also strengthened their in position. This change in the policy of the state towards these grantees enabled them to increase their influence in their respective areas. Similarly it also made the grantees fairly strong socially. With this farman a source of livelihood was assured.

In 1672–3 Aurangzeb ordered the resumption of all *madad-i-maash* grants of non-Muslims.[73] However, this order was not motivated by the idea of religious persecution of Hindus, as Aurangzeb is commonly and frequently charged. He has the image of temple destroyer. These views could hardly be accepted in the light of historical evidences now available.

Some of Aurangzeb's actions should not be seen in isolation. In order to appreciate his views and policy towards non-Muslims, a study of the political developments during his reign is essential for a perspective. It may be mentioned that from 1663 to 1679 Shivaji kept the Mughal empire under increasing pressure.[74] The condition of Marwar in 1679 after the death of Jaswant Singh created a serious problem for Mughal rule and the reimposition of *jazia* in the same year was certainly a symbolic expression of the reassertion of Mughal power. Similarly the Jat rebellion in 1669 and the Satnami rebellion in 1672 were followed by the royal orders for the demolition of the Kashi Vishwanath temple in 1669 and the Keshav Rai temple of Mathura in 1670.

About the same period, a farman was issued for revoking *madad-i-maash* grants of the non-Muslims. However, it seems that this farman was simply a threat to the defiant elements among the non-Muslims and a preventive measure. It is doubtful whether the order was actually made operative, as there is no evidence to confirm that lands reverted to the state on the basis of this farman. On the contrary, there are a number of references to grants of the Hindu *madad-i-maash* holders being confirmed and renewed from 1672–3 onwards.[75]

On the whole it can be observed that Aurangzeb made no material change in the system of assignment of *madad-i-maash* grants, nor did he reverse the earlier policy drastically. He helped in the growth of *madad-i-maash* holders as a distinct class.

After Aurangzeb the Mughal power declined. The administrative problems such as crisis in agrarian and *jagirdari* systems did not permit the state to pay attention to other affairs. As far as the institution of *madad-i-maash* grant was concerned, no major change was made in its administration. In 1722 Awadh emerged as an independent province under the governorship of Nawab Saadat Khan. He started to consoldiate the province of Awadh. Saadat Khan adopted the policy of subjugation of defiant elements of the suba. He compelled the defiant zamindars of the suba to accept his supermacy.[76] Later he paid attention to activities of the *madad-i-maash* holders. He found that the grantees had become one of the powerful groups of the suba and therefore he adopted a policy to establish his authority over them. In the beginning Saadat Khan was very strict towards the *madad-i-maash* holders. He began to review and resume *madad-i-maash* grants of such assignees whose record was not satisfactory.[77]

It may be mentioned here that *madad-i-maash* grants of only those grantees of the suba were recalled who posed a threat to the authority of the nawab. He patronized and favoured those grantees who were loyal and were peaceable.[78] For instance the grant of Mulla Nizamud-din of pargana Sahali in sarkar Lucknow was renewed.[79] However, the resumption of the grants of some of the assignees indicate that nawab intended to enforce his power over them and to compel them to remain loyal to him. But over the long term, the nawab could not succeed. Grantees such as the *qazi* of Bilgram made representations in the Mughal court and succeeding in gaining the intervention of Mughal emperor. Those who could not be represented in the imperial court had to follow the order of the nawab. Moreover, the nawab continued the policy of reviewing the performance of *madad-i-maash* grantees.[80] Thus it can be pointed out that from the time of Saadat Khan the *madad-i-maash* holders became more dependent on provincial authorities.

Safdarjang and Shuja-ud-Daula adopted a relatively generous policy towards *madad-i-maash* holders. The relations between the grantees and the nawabs remained cordial. It may be mentioned that generally the *madad-i-maash* holders who became economically sound, had acquired *zamindari* rights in the eighteenth century. This must have also contributed towards the adoption of a liberal policy by the nawabs. The nawabs intended to create a new class of zamindars by giving concessions to these grantees in converting *madad-i-maash* assignments into the *zamindaris.* It seems that the nawabs wanted to use this new class of zamindars against the old and defiant zamindars of the suba. This helped *madad-i-maash* holders who had recently acquired *zamindari* rights to become relatively powerful. Now the state did not treat *madad-i-maash* grants as an article of loan (*ariyat*), but as an article of proprietary right (*milkiyat*). This the basic nature and purpose of *madad-i-maash* grant underwent a radical change because of political expediency.

It may be concluded that during Akbar's reign the state intended to create a class of *madad-i-maash* holders as a socio-religious need and the grantees were not allowed to interfere in political matters. Jahangir recognized them as a distinct social group offering prayer and watching the interest of the State. This policy continued more or less in the same spirit up to Aurangzeb. However, the *madad-i-maash* holders in due course became a powerful group both socially and politically in their respective areas. When Awadh became as an independent suba, the nawabs also adopted the same policy but wanted the grantees to be more loyal to them than to the central authority.

NOTES

1. *Ain.*, vol. II (English trans.), pp. 167–336.
2. It may be mentioned that Akbar had made certain administrative reforms in the organization of the army and land revenue: The revision of branding of horses (*dagh* system) and introduction of *mansabdari* system and the classification of lands and collection of land revenue according to the fertility of land. The reforms in *madad-i-maash* institution were a part of Akbar's administrative reforms.
3. Those who had withdrawn from all worldly occupation and made no difference beteen night and day time in searching after true knowledge. Ibid., vol. I (English trans.), p. 278.
4. Those who practised self-denial and were engaged in the struggle with selfish passions of human nature. They had renounced society. Ibid.
5. They were economically so weak that they could not earn their livelihood. Ibid.
6. Persons of noble lineage who had lost their occupation for some reason. Ibid.
7. S.A.A. Rizvi, *Religious and Intellectual History of the Muslims in Akbar's Reign*, Delhi, 1978, p. 168.
8. It was customary during the medieval period for a new king to make land grants as a gesture of goodwill to his subjects and favourites. In this connection R.P. Tripathi says, '. . . whenever therefore, a new dynasty came to power it had to confirm these grants and make its own contribution. Even Sher Shah Suri cancelled the old grants and issued them again in his own name and to his own followers.' *Rise and Fall of the Mughal Empire*, Allahabad, 1972, pp. 243–4. It can, therefore, be assumed that the resumption of the *madad-i-maash* grants of the Afghans during Akbar's reign was a continuation of the policy of his predecessor.

9. Akbar came to know that the grantees were involved in illegal practices. They occupied *madad-i-maash* grants in two or more places unlawfully. He therefore in 1578 ordered the concentration of grants in certain villages. Allahabad Document, No. 24, Uttar Pradesh State Archives, Allahabad. Irfan Habib, *Agrarian System of Mughal India*, Bombay, 1963, p. 302.
10. *Ain.*, vol. I (English trans.), p. 279.
11. For example a large number of the grantees planted orchards on their land to enhance their income. S.A.A. Rizvi, *Religious and Intellectual History of the Muslims in Akbar's Reign*, p. 169.
12. *Ain.*, vol. I (English trans.), p. 279.
13. Ibid.
14. Shaikh Abdur Rashidi, '*Sayurghal* Lands Under the Mughals', in H.R. Gupta (ed.), *Essays Presented to Sir J.N. Sarkar*, Hoshiarpur, 1958, p. 318.
15. *Ain.*, vol. I (English trans.), p. 279.
16. Ibid.
17. Ibid.
18. Ibid.
19. Ibid.
20. Ibid., pp. 279–80.
21. The terms *uftada* and *mazru* have been used for cultivable waste land. Irfan Habib, *Agrarian System*, p. 302.
22. *Ain.*, vol. I (English trans.), p. 280.
23. The *qazis* were judicial officers, also connected with the administration of *madad-i-maash* grants.
24. *Ain.*, vol. I (English trans.), p. 279.
25. Ibid.
26. The *sadr-us-sudur* was head of the *madad-i-maash* grant institution. During Akbar's region the *sadr* was ranked as the fourth officer of the empire. He was the highest law officer and incharge of all lands devoted to ecclesiastical and benevolent purposes. Ibid., p. 281.
27. Ibid.
28. The six *sadrs* of Akbar's reign were Shaikh Gadai, Khwaja Muhammad Salih, Shaikh Abdunai, Sultan Khawaja, Amir Fatehullah and Sadr-i-Jahan.
29. Iqtedar Alam Khan, 'The Nobility Under Akbar and the Development of His Religious Policy (1560–80)', *Journal of the Royal Asiatic Society*, 1968, p. 30.
30. *Tuzuk-i-Jahangir*, translated by A. Rogers, Delhi, 1978, p. 10.
31. Ibid.
32. Jahangir mentions in his memoris, 'This year I awarded to the poor with my own hand and in my presence rupees fifty five thousand cash, one lac and ninety bighas of land, fourteen villages and twenty six ploughs and eleven thousand *kharwar* of rice.' Ibid., p. 279.
33. Ibid., p. 84.
34. Ibid., p. 10; also see Irfan Habib, *Agrarian System*, p. 310.
35. According to Irfan Habib, 'The term Lashkar-Duagon was apt because the

farmans of *madad-i-massh* usually contains a clause requiring the grantees to pray for enternal prosperity of the Empire', *Agrarian System*, p. 310.
36. Ibn Hasan, *Central Structure*, p. 270.
37. Employees of the shrine.
38. Iqbal Husain, '*Madad-i-Maash* Regulation in the Mughal Empire', PIHC, 1977, p. 305.
39. K.P. Srivastava (ed.), *Mughal Farmans (1540–1706)*, vol. I, Lucknow, 1974, p. 16, Doc. No. 9.
40. Iqbal Hasain, '*Madad-i-Maash* Regulation', PIHC, 1977, p. 305.
41. K.K. Dutta, *Some Mughal Farmans, Sanads, Parwanas*, Patna, 1962, p. 11.
42. K.P. Srivastava (ed.), *Mughal Farmans*, p. 16. Iqbal Husain, '*Madad-i-Maash* Regulation', PIHC, 1977, p. 307.
43. Ibid.
44. Ibid.
45. Compare Irfan Habib, *Agrarian System*, p. 308.
46. Ibid., p. 309.
47. Compare ibid.
48. Ibid., p. 308.
49. *Nankar* was a payment given to the zamindars in lieu of their revenue collection and military services.
50. *Malikana* right was paid to the zamindars for the maintenance of their families. It was given without any condition.
51. Compare Ibn Hasan, *Central Structure*, p. 225.
52. Ibid., p. 275.
53. Ibid. pp. 275–6.
54. *Jagirs* were the area of lands which revenue was enjoyed by the government officials, particularly military men.
55. Ibn Hasan, *Central Structure*, p. 276.
56. *Essays Presented to Sir J.N. Sarkar*, p. 321.
57. Ibn Hasan, *Central Structure*, p. 276.
58. Ibid., pp. 276–7.
59. Iqbal Husain, '*Madad-i-Maash* Regulation', PIHC, 1977, pp. 307–8.
60. Ibid., p. 308.
61. J.S. Grewal and B.N. Goswamy, *The Mughals and Jogis of Jakhbar*, pp. 115–16.
62. Iqbal Husain, '*Madad-i-Maash* Regulation', PIHC, 1977, p. 308.
63. Irfan Habib, *Agrarian System*, p. 304.
64. Muzaffar Alam, 'Some Aspects of the Changes in the Position of Madad-i-Maash holders in Awadh (1676–1772)', PIHC, 1974, p. 198.
65. The original grant was assigned during Shahjahan's reign, Allahabad Doc. No. 848.
66. The original grant was assigned during Jahangir reign. Ibid., No. 765.
67. In 1668 Shaikh Nurullah and others were renewed the *madad-i-maash* grant of 70 *bighas*, pargana and sarkar Bahraich, suba Awadh without any reduction in the size of grant assigned earlier. Allahabad Doc., No. 833. In 1669, 302 *bighas*

of grant was renewed in favour of Sayyid Jamaluddin in pargana and sarkar Bahraich, suba Awadh without making any changes in the size of originally assigned grant. Ibid., No. 767. In 1670 heirs of Mst. Raj Gosain were renewed whole grant of 200 *bighas* in pargana Fakhrpur, sarkar Bahraich. Ibid., No. 631.

68. Iqbal Husain, '*Madad-i-Maash* Regulation', PIHC, 1977, p. 309.
69. Allahabad Doc., Nos. 53, 55.
70. Compare Irfan Habib, *Agrarian System*, p. 306; K.P. Srivastava, *Mughal Farmans*, pp. 70–1.
71. Irfan Habib, *Agrarian System*, p. 309.
72. K.P. Srivastava, *Mughal Farmans*, p. 71.
73. Francois Bernier, *Travels in Mogul Emprie*; translated by A. Constable, edited by V.A. Smith, London, 1916, p. 341.
74. Sir J.N. Sarkar, *Short History of Aurangzeb's Reign*, Calcutta, 1962, pp. 465–72.
75. K.K. Dutta, *Some Mughal Farmans, Sanads and Parwanas*, pp. 26, 30, 59, 67, 68, 69, 73, 74, 75, 79 and 84.
76. For a detailed study of the relation of Nawab Saadat Khan with the zamindars, see A.L. Srivastava, *First Two Nawabs*.
77. Muzaffar Alam, *The Crisis of Empire in Mughal North India: Awadh and the Punjab 1707–1748*, Delhi, 1986, p. 220.
78. Manzar Hasan Gilani, *Hindustan Mein Musalmano ka Nizam-i-Taalim*, vol. I, Delhi, 1966, pp. 278–9.
79. Mufti Raza Ansari, *Bani-i-Dars-i-Nizami*, Aligarh, 1973, pp. 64–86.
80. Allahabad Doc., No. 117. Muzaffar Alam, *The Crisis of Empire*, p. 223.

CHAPTER 3

Procedure and Nature of *Madad-i-Maash* Grants

PROCEDURE

The procedure for the assignment of a *madad-i-maash* grants was by no means simple. It could be conferred only after completion of a number of formalities. The recipient first made a request to the *sadr-us-sudur*. The *sadr-us-sudur* made enquiry whether the applicant was eligible to be considered for any of the categories permissible for the assignment of such a grant.[1] When found suitable he was asked by the *sadr* or other competent authority to appear before the emperor.[2] This process was called *fard-i-haqiqat*.[3]

After the emperor's approval, details like the name of the *sadr* and the name of the *waqia nigar*[4] were recorded in the *yadasht-i-waqia*.[5] On completion of these formalities the *yadasht*[6] was again presented before the emperor by the *sadr* for confirmation of his approval. This process was called *arz-i-mukarrar*.[7]

After completion of the *arz-i-mukarrar*, orders were issued to prepare the farman for the assignment of the *madad-i-maash* grant.[8] This process was called the *sarkhat*.[9] The farman was drafted in the office of the diwan. After the preparation the farman was signed by the *mustaufi*[10] and entered in the office of the *diwan-i-saadat*. Then it was signed and sealed by the *sadr* and *diwan-i-kul*.[11]

In the farman the specifications and size of *madad-i-maash* land, the name of the grantee and necessary instruction to the official of the area concerned were recorded. It was also instructed that the *madad-i-maash* land as mentioned in the farman be handed over to the grantee.[12] Other details of *madad-i-maash* grant were recorded on the reverse called *zimn*.[13] After the completion of these formalities, a farman relating to *madad-i-maash* grant was deemed to be complete.

To make the farman granting the *madad-i-maash* assignment operative a parwana was issued normally by the *sadr*. However, it could be issued by other officials also, duly authorized for the purpose.[14] This order (parwana) reproduced the content of the farman. It was handed over to officials such as *gumashtas*,[15] *karoris*[16] and *mutasaddis*[17] for compliance.[18]

Such grants were also given by the prince, princess and queens. Such documents were called *nishan*.[19] But the number of such extant orders are few as compared to those issued by the emperor.

When the *madad-i-maash* grant was confirmed, special order was issued which was known as *farman-i-sabiti*.[20] It was signed by the many officials of the state, including the *wakil*, *mushrif-i-diwan*, *sadr-us-sudur*, *mir-i-mal*, *khan-i-saman*, *bakhshi*, *nazir*, *diwan-i-buyyat* and *diwan-i-kul*, etc.[21] The *farman-i-sabiti* had generally a round seal, the *muhr-i-uzak*.[22] This document had five folds. On the first fold the *wakil* put his seal, on the second the *mushrif-i-diwan*, on the third the *sadr's* seal was stamped, and on the fourth and fifth the seals of *mushrif* and *sahib-i-taujib* respectively.[23]

The farman began with some Koranic verses in the name of God.[24] On the right of the farman, the *tughra* was put which bore the name of the emperor. Generally the text consisted of the following:[25]

> The date of the assignment of the grant, the area of *madad-i-maash* lands, the name of the pargana, sarkar and suba, the name of the grantee, the order of demarcation and measurement, whether taxable or non-taxable, instruction for renewal, and the date and year of the issue of the farman.

The text of the farman was followed by an endorsement on the *zimn*. The endorsement comprised the following details:[26]

> Farman issued through the register (*risala*) of the official concerned, the name of the caligraphist, the seals of the different officials, and the name of the co-sharer of the grant and the size of the holdings assigned to each grantee.

Generally the farmans and parwanas were addressed to the *gumashtas* of jagirdars, *mutasaddis* and *karoris* of the place where the *madad-i-maash* land was assigned.[27] But some farmans were also addressed to other officials like the *shiqdar*[28] and *muqaddams*.[29]

When all the required information for the documents were completed, the officials concerned measured[30] and demarcated the assigned lands. Finally a *chaknama*[31] was issued to the grantee, authorizing him to cultivate the assigned land.[32]

It may be noted that the above-mentioned formalities were completed at the time of assignment of an original *madad-i-maash* grant. Moreover, at the time of renewal, the grantee had to produce a number of witnesses in favour of his claim. When it was found that the grantee was in actual possession and had no other means of livelihood, the assigned *madad-i-maash* grant was renewed.

Thus, from the time of the emperor's approval to the issuing of farman and assigning of the *madad-i-maash* grant, there were a number of formalities to be completed.

NATURE OF THE *MADAD-I-MAASH* GRANTS

Madad-i-maash holders were given many concessions, but the state fixed certain rules and regulations, meant to protect the grantees from exploitation at the hand of officials and also to impose certain restrictions to prevent the grantees from illegal encroachment. The nature of *madad-i-maash* grants included several considerations as regards rights of the grantees on the assigned lands.

The *madad-i-maash* grant was revenue free. All royal imposts were exempted from the grantees. In the *madad-i-maash* documents it is clearly indicated that the grantees should be exempted from all *wujuhat*, *awaridat*, *mal-o-jihat* and *ikhrajat*.[33] However, it may be pointed out that the grant was not always rent-free, as its holders had to pay local and customary taxes. Some references indicate that after 1650 some taxes were collected from the grantees of the suba of Awadh. A document of pargana Haveli Bahraich shows that cases like *zamindari*,[34] *chaudharai*,[35] *qanungoi*, *nambardari*,[36] *khewat*,[37] *mehmani*[38] and *sadrana*[39] were realized from the grantees in 1698–9.[40] Another document of pargana Amethi shows that the *madad-i-maash* holders of Amethi paid *behri*[41] tax to the state officials.[42] Moreover, the officials also collected some illegal taxes from the grantees. During Aurangzeb's reign, Shivdas, qanungo of pargana Haveli Bahraich realized some *abwab*[43] in respect of his perquisite from the grantee Mir Sayyid Ahmed.[44] In 1665 an official realized Rs. 7,185 from the *aimmadars* of Amethi.[45] It may be mentioned that state officials were repeatedly instructed not to collect illegal taxes from grantees, and there ware references to show that whenever a grantee made complaints about illegal demands, the state ordered for refunds.[46] However, such representations against the concerned officials were possible only for the influential or a group of *madad-i-maash* holders. Grantees who were not economically or socially strong suffered at the hands of the local officials.

The imposition of cesses on *madad-i-maash* holders seems to have started in the second half of the seventeenth century.[47] Since the beginning of eighteenth century, the cessesment on *madad-i-maash* land became a common practice. The conditions for the imposition of these cesses varied from grantee to grantee. Cesses were imposed on the land of those who had large holdings. It was perhaps in view of this fact that over a period of time the uncultivated portion of the land assigned also became cultivated and productive. Therefore the surplus increased considerably, which was of advantage to grantee and state alike—the intended to share a part of increased surplus of the grantees. It needs to be mentioned that cesses were imposed mostly on those grantees who produced large yields. Thus cesses imposed on such holders did not cause much hardship. Even so, they were strongly resented.

As far as the collection of illegal cess is concerned, it was also connected with the improved economic condition of the grantees. Those who were given *madad-i-maash* lands for their livelihood, in due course became economically well off, therefore the officials started to collect some taxes from them as their perquisite. However, it may be mentioned that the cesses imposed on the *madad-i-maash* holders were less as than those for other landed aristocrats.

Madad-i-maash land was assigned on both conditional and unconditional basis. In the suba of Awadh a large part of *madad-i-maash* land was assigned to the *sadrs, qazis, mutuwallis,*[48] *sajjada nashin*[49] and other officials concerned with religio-judicial functions. Such grants were in lieu of salaries. Some other persons were also assigned conditional *madad-i-maash* land in lieu of services to society, for instance, in 1578 Akbar issued a general farman to the officials of the parganas that the *madad-i-maash* land should be exclusively assigned to holy persons in a few villages independent of *khalsa* and *jagir* lands; these persons should be instructed to build a mosque, house, *chaupal* and garden in the villages where they settled.[50] Many references indicate that *madad-i-maash* lands were assigned for the construction of wells and mosques for the help of travellers, students, and the needy.[51]

Unconditional *madad-i-maash* grants were given to those who did not perform a duty for the state. However, such grantees were expected to pray for the everlasting empire. They were also expected to get social support of the people in favour of the state. These grant holders had not other means of livelihood. This led to the creation of a group of persons who remained totally dependent on the state for their survival. Through them, on the one hand, the state projected its generosity towards the needy and learned; on the other hand, members of this class with their roots among the local people watched the interest of the state. Thus unconditional grant holders also rendered valuable service to the state. However, the main difference between conditional and unconditional grants was only that the latter were free from any specific duty, but helped the state derive support for itself from the people of the respective areas.

Generally *madad-i-maash* lands were assigned in certain numbers of *bighas*. In some cases grants also consisted of entire villages. The size of *madad-i-maash* holdings, therefore, varied from grantee to grantee.

In the suba of Awadh there were many grantees who possessed more than 200 *bighas* of land.[52] Some grantees were given 1,000 *bighas* or even more.[53] Some grantees were assigned entire villages as *madad-i-maash*.[54] On the other hand there were also a large number of grantees who held quite small holdings which varied from 4 to 50 *bighas* of land.

The size of the holding did not affect the purpose of such grants or the duties of the grant holder, but it certainly affected social status. For instance, in view of their special functions, conditional grant holders such as *sajjada nashin*, *qazis*, *mutawallis* and *muftis* were given generally large areas of land.

As stated, *madad-i-maash* land consisted of both cultivated and uncultivated-but-cultivable land. Generally half the land assigned was from each category. This was with a view to bring more and more uncultivated lands under the plough.

Normally *madad-i-maash* land was assigned in consolidated form. An assignee was given his whole grant in a particular village.[55] However, in some cases *madad-i-maash* land was also given in scattered plots, in more than one village.[56] Some grantees were even assigned land in more than one pargana.[57] It seems that the grant was given in scattered form with a view to preventing the grantees from increasing their hold in a particular area, which was likely to create law and order problems. This is confirmed by the fact that the lands to big grant holders were mostly given scattered in different areas.[58] But in cases where the duties of a *madad-i-maash* holder related to different areas, the state made the scattered allocations to suit his convenience. As the work of *qazis* related to different villages, they were assigned new land in different villages. For example, in Aurangzeb's reign Qazi Imad-ud-din had pargana Sandila, sarkar Lucknow and pargana Nimkhar sarkar Khairabad under his jurisdiction. He was assigned his *madad-i-maash* land accordingly.[59] Thus it seems that often the places of the assignment of *madad-i-maash* land was in the vicinity of the region where the grantee was appointed.

After 1690 a major change in the nature of *madad-i-maash* assignments is noticeable: the grants were made hereditary. This practice continued and hardly any evidence is available where the grant of a family was cancelled in the suba of Awadh during the seventeenth and eighteenth centuries. If the grantee was loyal his assignment was confirmed to his heirs. Therefore it may be found that in the suba of Awadh the *madad-i-maash* holders retained land generation after generation.[60] In 1658 Mir Sayyid Ahmed inherited a *madad-i-maash* grant that had originally been assigned during Akbar's reign in pargana Haveli and sarkar Bahraich.[61] Sayyid Jamal-ud-Din of pargana Haveli and sarkar Bahraich got renewed his grant of 267 *bighas* and 19 *biswas* in 1665, this grant was originally assigned to his family in Akbar's reign.[62] In view of the documents available, the evidence of such practice could be easily multiplied.[63]

In the time of Nawab Saadat Khan Burhan-ul-Mulk, the first nawab (1722–39) of Awadh, the policy began of the confiscation of *madad-i-maash* land,[64] but not in the whole suba.[65] Numerous *madad-i-maash* holders retained their grants. It seems that Saadat Khan intended to discontinue the grants of the powerful assignees who were defiant or could be a threat to him. However, he did not succeed in his efforts, as the dissatisfied grantees made complaints against him in the court of Emperor Muhammad Shah (1719–48), who ordered Saadat Khan to restore the lands. The legitimization of the hereditary rights of the grantees over *madad-i-maash* lands by the central government forced the provincial authorities to recognize the claim of the heirs of the *madad-i-maash* holders.

However, despite the acceptance of the hereditary claim over their assigned land, the heirs had to have their grants confirmed and renewed in their favour. For this purpose a *madad-i-maash* had to prove that he was the real heir of the deceased grantee,[66] and had no other means of his livelihood.[67] In actual practice it seems that other means of livelihood did not debar a person from a *madad-i-maash* grant. This is established by *madad-i-maash* documents that record that if a grantee had other property apart from his *madad-i-maash* land anywhere else, it should be ignored.[68]

The confirmation of a grant were made under the following circumstances:

On the accession of a new emperor; when a *madad-i-maash* holder died; and if the officials concerned had any doubt regarding the claim of the grantee over his *madad-i-maash* grant.

No specific timings were prescribed by the state for such verification of documents for confirmation. It could be practised once, or any number of times during the lifetime of the granteee. However, in the case of the grantees of the suba of Awadh, the evidence shows that grantees had to get confirmation of their *madad-i-maash* grants more than once.[69] It may be mentioned that these confirmations were made in addition to the causes mentioned above.

In the absence of any specific procedure in terms of period for verifiation of documents, grantees were put to great hardship. Often it was difficult to satisfy officials about the claims at the time of the confirmation of grants. Consequently, *madad-i-maash* holders suffered at the hands of state officials.[70]

Sometimes it led to conflict between the *madad-i-maash* holders and the state officials and were solved only with the intervention of the court.[71]

The renewal of the grant was done only after its confirmation, and by the *sadr*.[72] In this connection his views were considered most authentic. At the time of renewal the shares of all claimants or co-sharers were determined.[73] Here it may be mentioned that the area of the *madad-i-maash* land was measured by the *illahi qaz*.[74]

The grounds for the confirmation and renewal during the closing years of the seventeenth century underwent a change. According to the farman of 1690, Aurangzeb approved the hereditary rights of *madad-i-maash* holders. In the light of this farman the *aimma* land was to be confirmed to the heirs of the deceased without change.[75] This obviously destroyed the very purpose of the assignment of *madad-i-maash* land, because now the merit of the heirs had no importance; the grants were renewed because of their being successors or relations of the original assignee. Owing to such confirmation and renewal the purpose of assigning such grants must have also been affected. On the decision that the *madad-i-maash* grant should be confirmed in the names of the members of families of the original *madad-i-maash* holders, the possibility of assignment to undeserving persons would have increased. Claims for confirmation and renewal in favour of a particular person now depended on the wishes of the original grantees. And as such there was no need for the verification of the claims for the renewal of the grant. If the original grantee did not declare his or her heirs, any member of his family could apply for the renewal. Even persons who were economically strong could claim renewal in their favour. It is evident from *madad-i-maash* documents that after the death of the original grantee a number of persons claimed to be the real heirs of the deceased.[76] Since there was no fixed state law to examine the validity of their claim, the grant was divided among all the claimants. Such pattern of renewal of the grant created problems for both the state and the grantees. Therefore the eligibility for renewal of a *madad-i-maash* grant was determined by a candidate's association with the family of the *madad-i-maash* holder. This led to misuse of the grants; those who had sufficient economic backing too became *madad-i-maash* holders being heirs or relations of deceased grantees. The grant were renewed not according to need, but according to the claims. Consequently a person often inherited the grants of many grantees. If there were many *madad-i-maash* holders in a family, but it had only one heir, the grants of all family members were renewed in favour of a particular claimant. This increased the areas of the *madad-i-maash* lands under a grantee. Gradually these *madad-i-maash* holders acquired practically the *zamindari* rights with sufficient economic base and political strength. They violated the rules and regulations and consequently came in conflict with the other sections of landed aristocracy.[77]

In many cases there were a number of claimants for the renewal of a particular *madad-i-maash* grant. Therefore, the whole grant of such a grantee was divided among a number of claimants. This kind of division of grants led to the creation of small and scattered holdings.[78] The small and scattered holdings were obviously less beneficial for agricultural purposes. Thus the division of grants into a number of shareholders were against the interest of agricultural growth. Besides, the small holdings, the division of large areas into many shareholders created disputes among the co-sharers of *madad-i-maash* land.[79] Sometimes a claimant was deprived of his rightful claims. In 1758–9 Sayyid Muhammad Azam forcibly seized the land assigned as *madad-i-maash* to Farugh Ali in pargana Mallawan, sarkar Lucknow. By misrepresentation he claimed one-third of the grant for confirmation in his favour. Although an enquiry was set-up to settle the dispute between Muhammad Azam and Farugh Ali, but latter could not get his entire grant confirmed in his favour.[80] Such cases gave an opportunity to the official concerned to make an illegal exaction. Normally the disputed cases were settled in the office of the *qazi*, and most of the *qazis* were involved in illegal practices of taking bribes from the petitioners and forcibly occupying the land of the others.[81] It was thus very difficult for the grantees to settle disputes without their help. Often the grantees could not get justice from other officials against the decision of the influential *qazi.* Therefore, the disgruntled grantees had to approach the emperor, if they were in a position to do so and a petition would in any case not be effective for a decision without the concurrence of the officials of the judicial department at local level. Since all officials of judicial department were closely associated with the *qazis,* they were bound to protect the latter. Thus it can be assumed that in the absence of any fixed rule regarding the confirmation and renewal of grants after the close of the seventeenth century many problems were created for both the grantees and the state.

Normally a *madad-i-maash* grant could be resumed, reduced, increased and transferred. The *Ain-i-Akbari* mentions that if a grant had been made to a group of people without specifiying their shares in the *zimn* of the farman and any one of them died, the *sadr* had to determine the share of deceased grantee. His share was to be declared *khalsa* land until the heir represented his claim at court.[82]

Aurangzeb also issued orders regarding the conditions under which grants could be reduced or resumed by the state. These orders have been recorded in the parwana of Raja Raghunath dated 10 January 1661.[83]

It specifies:

(i) If the grantee died and left behind a wife or son, daughter or sons of the daughter, and the *madad-i-maash* grant assigned to him was equal to 30 *bighas* or less, the whole grant should be confirmed to him;

(ii) In case the land grant exceeded the limit of 30 *bighas,* half of the same should be resumed and the remaining half should be assigned to his heir or heirs.

(iii) If the heirs were not satisfied with the reduced grant they could make petition in the royal court and if they presented satisfactory evidence regarding their claim against the reduction of the grant the reduction was to be restored.

(iv) If the grantee died and his document of grant mentioned the term 'ba Farzandan'[84] after his name, then one half of the grant was to be confirmed in favour of his heirs, otherwise the whole grant was to be resumed.

(v) If the grantee held a valid document at the time of the accession of Aurangzeb he retained the assigned grant, but in the cases of such grantees who died after his accession and had more than 20 *bighas* as *madad-i-maash* lands, half of its was to be resumed. However, if they had less than 20 *bighas* the same was to be restored to their heirs

These orders indicate that the state reserved its right to confiscate and reduce grant. In the subas of Bihar and Lahore some grants were affected by these orders.[85] However, in the suba of Awadh these orders were not implemented, perhaps because there was no cause of such an action by the state.

There is hardly any evidence for the resumption of *madad-i-maash* grants in Awadh. Generally the entire *madad-i-maash* lands of the grantee were renewed for heirs.[86]

The farman of Aurangzeb of 1681–2 completely changed the rule of resumption and reduction of *madad-i-maash*. According to this farman, 'All grants already made should be continued without any change diminution in the names of the heirs of the deceased and in the case of such heirs who already held other grants, the shares in those grants should be acknowledged and that should be considered as an additional grants.[87] It is evident from a number of *madad-i-maash* documents that this regulation was followed during Aurangzeb's reign and throughout the eighteenth century. However, the privilege of the continuation of the entire grant was extended to the grantees so long as they remained loyal to the state. Rebellion could deprive them of their grants. This is confirmed by the fact that Nawab Saadat Khan of Awadh revoked the grants of rebellious holders.[88] However, it seems that in the suba of Awadh, the bulk of the grantees enjoyed the above-mentioned concessions in view of their continued loyalty.

There was no prescribed rule regarding the increase in the area of the grants. This depended on the will of the emperor and other state authorities. It seems from some cases that the sizes of holdings were increased when found in sufficient for the requirements of the grantee. For instance, in 1677 Qazi Imad-ud-Din was assigned 10 *bighas* for laying out a garden, construction of a *khanqah* and a well. In 1684 he found that 10 *bighas* were not sufficient for the purpose, and the allotment was increased from 10 to 17 *bighas*.[89] Moreover, the area of the grants of conditional *madad-i-maash* holders could also be increased when the official concerned was assigned additional duties. For instance, during Aurangzeb's reign Imad-ud-Din was appointed *qazi* in pargana Sandila, sarkar Lucknow. After a while he was also given the duties of *muhatasib* and *nirkh navis*.[90] Consequently the area of his *madad-i-maash* land was increased.[91] The areas were also increased when grantees were assigned public office, generally religio-judicial duties. In case of assigning extra duties to any such member, an additional *madad-i-maash* grant was sanctioned as a conditional grant to him.

Land assigned for additional duties as conditional grant was essentially cultivated land and normally less than the area of the original grant. It seems that this practice was encouraged by the state, because if the grant was given afresh to a new person for a particular task the size would have to be larger. Through this practice the state could assign *madad-i-maash* lands to more and more persons for additional duties without the need of increased areas of cultivated land. As such the original assignees were happy to get additional cultivated land. This was found beneficial for both state and grantee.

The practice of increasing the size of *madad-i-maash* holdings became more common after Aurangzeb's death. Due to obvious reasons the grantees aspired for larger size of holdings under their control. The eighteenth century witnessed great political instability contributing to the decline of Mughal empire and the emergence of the local and regional powers. The *madad-i-maash* holders due to their local position became considerably strong in their respective areas and found an opportunity to increase the size of their grants illegally. Imperial orders began to be defied.

Madad-i-maash land could be transferred from one place to another under special situations. In case *madad-i-maash* holders were harassed by local people and found themselves unable to utilize the assigned lands, they could request for a transfer of their grants to other areas evidence regarding such requests is more common in the suba of Awadh after 1650.[92] There were also provisions for the exchange of *madad-i-maash* lands on mutual agreement between assignees.[93] It appears that the welfare and satisfaction of grantees was the main consideration behind such transfers from one place to another. The state wanted to assign lands to grantees at the place where they may not be victimized by local people. If there was any apprehension that a particular assignment of *madad-i-maash* grant was likely to create a law and order problem and the grantee was likely to suffer at the hands of local people, his assignment was transferred.

The *madad-i-maash* holders were expected to enjoy only the revenue of the lands assigned to them, and officially had no proprietary rights on their grants; hence they were prevented by the state from acquiring *milikiyat* rights.[94] They were aksed to pay the *malikana* share to the zamindar.[95] A document of Aurangzeb's reign indicates that the *madad-i-maash* lands were not alienable (*qabil-i-tamlik nist*).[95] The farman issued by Aurangzeb in 1692 defines *madad-i-maash* grants held on loans (*ariyat*).[97] All this indicates that *madad-i-maash* lands were assigned on a non-proprietary basis. But in practice the *madad-i-maash* holders always treated *madad-i-maash* lands as their property.[98]

In the suba of Awadh too, the *madad-i-maash* holders increasingly tried to establish their proprietary rights (*malikana*), specifically denied by the state. Gradually they acquired *zamindari* rights illegally over their *madad-i-maash* lands. In the last years of Aurangzeb's reign the *madad-i-maash* holders of the suba of Awadh sold and leased out their lands. In 1672 Mir Muhammad Ahmed, a grantee of pargana Haveli and sarkar Bahraich, purchased *zamindari* right of a village.[99] Another *madad-i-maash* holder Muhammad Arif of pargana Haveli purchased *zamindari* rights of several villages in the years 1681, 1687, 1688 and 1689.[100] There are some other references which indicate that grantees in Awadh did not treat *madad-i-maash* lands as held on *ariyat*, but acquired *milkiyat* rights.[101]

Thus it is clear that the *madad-i-maash* grant had undergone a change in late seventeenth century and more particularly in the eighteenth century. The *madad-i-maash* grant which was for a specific purpose and for people of particular professions, was essentially an arrangement to help the learned, needy and those engaged in religious pursuits. In making these grants the state originally wanted to provide support. There was no intention to make grants hereditary if the concerned grantees seized to function satisfactorily. Thus from the very beginning the nature of assignment of the *madad-i-maash* grants were conditional on the needs of a person and his loyalty to the state. As such the *madad-i-maash* grant was directly linked with work and performance and it could only remain valid while the grantee discharged his duties to the satisfaction of the state. However, over a period of time *madad-i-maash* grants not only became hereditary, but the grantees became owners of the lands. They acquired *zamindari* rights, purchased additional areas, and even occupied areas forcibly. Thus not only was the purpose for which the *madad-i-maash* lands assigned negated, but *madad-i-maash* holders acquired much political clout at the local and regional levels.

NOTES

1. Persons of four categories such as poor, saints, scholars and noble birth who had lost their occupation.
2. The *sadr* presented needy of *madad-i-maash* grants at *Jharokha* and *Gusalkhana* assemblies. R.M. Bilgrami, *Religious and Quasi Religious Departments of Mughal Period*, Delhi, 1984, p. 66.

3. *Farhanq-i-Kardani*, Abdus Salam Collection 85/135, Maulana Azad Library, Aligarh Muslim University, Aligarh, F. 39a.
4. *Waqia nigar*: a recorder of events or news writer, 'an official who kept a record of the various orders issued by and transactions connected with the sovereign'.
5. *Yadasht-i-waqia*: official record.
6. *Yadasht*: Memorandum.
7. N.A. Siddiqui, *Land Revenue Administration, Under the Mughals (1700–1750)*, Bombay, 1970, p. 170.
8. Ibid., p. 127.
9. R.M. Bilgrami, *Religious and Quasi Religious Departments*, p. 67.
10. *Mustaufi*: an auditor of accounts.
11. *Ain.*, vol. I (English trans.), p. 273.
12. Allahabad Doc. No. 222.
13. Some references indicate that during Akbar's reign and to 1578 the areas of *madad-i-maash* grants were given in the text. N.A. Siddiqui, *Land Revenue Administration*, p. 127.
14. For instance in 1659 Nawab Diler Khan issued parwana for the assignment of 450 *bighas* of *madad-i-maash* grants to Qazi Habibullah and others in pargana Sandila, sarkar Lucknow, suba Awadh. National Archives of India, Doc. No. 1624. In 1665 Nawab Diler Khan issued a *parwana* to assign grants to Abdul Fath and Abdul Satar in pargana Sandila, sarkar Lucknow. Ibid., 2578, 2608/8. In 1730 Burhan-ul-Mulk Saadat Khan, nawab of Awadh, issued a parwana for the grant of land to Abul Khair in pargana Darybad, sarkar and suba Awadh. Allahabad Doc. No. 32.
15. *Gumashtas*: agents of the jagirdars.
16. *Karoris*: revenue collectors.
17. *Mutasaddis*: officers appointed to assist in the collection of revenue and the maintenance of law and order.
18. N.A. Siddiqui, *Land Revenue Administration*, p. 170.
19. In 1673 Prince Muhammad issued a *nishan* for the assignment of *madad-i-maash* grant in pargana Sandila, sarkar Lucknow, NAI, 1257. In 1674 he issued another *nishan* for the assignment of *madad-i-maash* lands to Muhammad Naim in pargana Sandila, sarkar Lucknow, ibid., 222. *Nishan* issued by the princess, see, Tirmizi—'A rare edicts of Nurjahan', *Proceedings of Indian Historical Record Commission*, vol. 35, pt. II, pp. 196–7.
20. *Ain.*, vol. I (English trans.), p. 271.
21. Ibid., pp. 271–3.
22. J.S. Grewal and B.N. Goswamy, *Mughals and Jogis of Jakhbar*, Simla, 1967.
23. R.M. Bilgrami, *Religious and Quasi Religious Departments*, p. 67.
24. Generally the Koranic verses used in farman were *Bismillah ir Rahman ir Rahim* (In the name of God, the merciful, the compassionate), *Atiullah Waatiur Rasul Wa Amir-i-minkun* (Obey God and obey the Prophet and those in authority among you) and *Allah-u-Akbar* (God is great), Allahabad Doc. No. 8, K.P. Srivastava, *Mughal Farmans*, Doc. No. 39.
25. Ibid., Doc. No. 38, NAI, Nos. 2157, 2159, Allahabad Doc. No. 32.

26. Allahabad Doc. No. 172; K.P. Srivastava, *Mughal Farmans*, Doc. Nos. 38, 39.
27. NAI, 1252, 1743, 2154 and 2157.
28. *Shiqdar*: head of the pargana.
29. NAI, 1742. *Muqaddam* was head of the village.
30. Generally *madad-i-maash* land was measured by *ilahiqaz*. Allahabad Doc. Nos. 9, 48 and 169.
31. *Chaknama*: a document showing the boundaries and area of assigned lands.
32. Allahabad Doc. Nos. 8, 796, 812, 815–1, 2 and 816–1, 2.
33. All state taxes. M.A. Ansari, *Administrative Documents*, Doc. Nos. 30, 31 and 39. Generally the taxes exempted from *madad-i-maash* lands were *guanlughah* (a gift made to the officers), *zabitana* (measurement tax), *muhassalana* (fees of the tax collectors), *paikar-o-shikar* (labour required from a peasant when the hunt was organized for a king or noble), *peshkash* (presents), *jaribana* (measurement fees), *muqaddami* (fee of the village headman), *qanungoi* (fee of the qanungo), *zabt-i-harsala* (annual assessment), *takrar-i-zirat* (burden on cultivation), *shuhnagi* (fee of the person who looked after the field) and *chitni* (fee on permission to cultivate the assigned land).
34. Fees of the zamindar.
35. Fees of the *chaudhari*.
36. Fees of the village headman.
37. A tax for village expenses.
38. Realized by the government officials.
39. Fees of *sadr*.
40. Allahabad Doc. Nos. 1177, 1204, 1230 and 1231.
41. A tax for digging well and other public works.
42. Allahabd Doc. Nos. 110 and 218.
43. An illegal exaction.
44. Allahabad Doc. No. 1212.
45. Ibid., No. 218.
46. Ibid.
47. N.A. Siddiqui, *Land Revenue Administration*, p. 124.
48. *Mutawalli* was an official concerned with the administration of *madad-i-maash* grants in the pargana.
49. *Sajjada nashin* was controller of the shrine.
50. Allahabad Doc. No. 24.
51. In 1675 Qazi Imad-ud-Din was assigned 294 *bighas* of *madad-i-maash* lands in the pargana Nimkhar, sarkar Khairabad, Suba Awadh for the maintenance of the shrine, poor and students. NAI, 1272. In 1678 he got another grant to meet the expenses of *khanqah*, ibid., 1373. In 1684 he was assigned 17 *bighas* of *madad-i-maash* lands to construct a mosque, *khanqah*, garden and well, ibid. 1651. In 1716 Shaikh Zain-ul-Abidin was assigned 4 *bighas* of *madad-i-maash* lands in pargana Haveli Gorakhpur, suba Awadh to lay out a garden to construct a well and a residential house, ibid. 2173 and 2447. In 1717 Syyid Karamullah was granted 235 *bighas* to meet the expenses of students, ibid., 1050.

52. Allahabad Doc. Nos. 32, 175, 250, 763, 764, 797, 834, 846, 848, 875; NAI, 1831, 2154, 2157, 2166 and 2171.
53. Allahabad Doc. Nos. 49 and 781.
54. Four villages were assigned to the *sajjada nashins* of the *khanqah* of Sayyid Ashraf Jahangir at different places in the suba of Awadh. Jais Doc. Nos. 2, 4, 5, 13, Department of History, AMU, Aligarh.
55. Allahabad Doc. Nos. 7, 822, 831, 847; NAI 1248, 1297, 1624, 2165 and 2578.
56. In 1610 Shaikh Habibullah was assigned 520 *bighas* of *madad-i-maash* lands in three villages of pargana Mallawan, sarkar Lucknow. Allahabad Doc. No. 36. In 1629 Jaffar was given his whole *madad-i-maash* lands in two villages of pargana Hisampur, sarkar Bahraich, ibid., p. 895. During Aurangzeb's reign, Qazi Habibullah was assigned *madad-i-maash* lands in many villages of pargana Sandila, sarkar Lucknow, NAI, 1270, 1296, 1228 and 1624.
57. During Aurangzeb's reign Muhammad Arif of sarkar Bahraich and Qazi Imad-ud-din of sarkar Lucknow were assigned *madad-i-maash* lands in more than one pargana. Allahabad Doc. Nos. 1202, 1228, 1230, 1231, NAI, 1272 and 1273.
58. Muhammad Arif of sarkar Bahraich possessed a large area as *madad-i-maash* lands. His *madad-i-maash* lands were scattered in diferent villages. Allahabad Doc. Nos. 764, 768, 856 and 1228.
59. NAI, 1360, 1393, 1434, 1747 and 1748.
60. Allahabad Doc. Nos. 765, 773, 775, 797, 798, 830, 883.
61. Ibid., 791.
62. Ibid., 760.
63. In 1669 Sayyid Muhammed Arif inherited the *madad-i-maash* lands of Sayyid Mashad which were originally granted during Jahangir's reign in pargana Haveli, sarkar Bahraich, suba Awadh. Allahabad Doc. No. 768. In 1670 some *bighas* were confirmed to the heirs of Mst. Raj Gosain which was originally assigned during Jaḥangir's reign in pargana Fatehpur, sarkar Lucknow, ibid., 831.
64. Muzaffar Alam, *The Crisis of Empire in Mughal North India: Awadh and the Punjab 1707–1748*, Delhi, 1986, p. 220.
65. In 1724, 131 *bighas* of *madad-i-maash* lands were confirmed to Shaikh Nurullah in pargana Sadrpur, sarkar Khairabad. Allahabad Doc. No. 854. In 1728 Shaikh Bayazid was confirmed his *madad-i-maash* grant in pargana Sandila, sarkar Lucknow. Ibid., No. 11. In 1732 Taj Muhammad, a *madad-i-maash* holder Daryabad, sarkar Awadh, was confimred his *madad-i-maash* grant. Ibid., No. 12.
66. Allahabad Doc. Nos. 7, 168, 170, 171, 172, 174, 766, 782, 806. Allahabad Doc. No. 169 indicates that 2,220 *bighas* of lands were confirmed to Mst. Bekhi and others in 1662 in pargana Hisampur, sarkar Bahraich when an enquiry was completed about her claim.
67. Allahabad Doc. Nos. 165, 166 and 168.
68. M.A. Ansari, *Administrative Documents*, Doc. Nos. 25, 27, 28 and 29.
69. The *madad-i-maash* grant of Sayyid Jamal-ud-Din was confirmed in the years of 1663, 1666, 1669, 1670, 1671 and 1688 in pargana Haveli and sarkar Bahraich. Allahabad Doc. Nos. 763, 767, 769, 797, 798, 844. The grant of Shaikh Daim

was confirmed in the years 1681, 1684, 1698 in pargana Sandila, sarkar Lucknow, NAI, 1422, 1440, 1435. There are several other references regarding multiplicity of the timings of the confirmation of the *madad-i-maash* grant. Ibid. 1345, 1409, 1443 and 1576.

70. In 1663 two brothers, Sadullah and Zain-ul-Abidin, petitioned the royal court that village Palhari was assigned as *madad-i-maash* to their father, Shaikh Budan, in pargana Kara Kilai, sarkar Bahraich during the reign of Shahjahan. But at the time of renewal of the grant in 1663, the *sadr* confiscated 500 *bighas* of land without giving a reason. Allahabad Doc. No. 1187.
71. According to M.A. Ansari, 'The *madad-i-maash* holders quite often failing in their efforts to convince the local or provincial office proceeded to the court, where they were able to get their grievances through a dignatory'. *Administrative Documents*, p. 24.
72. Sometimes the confirmation of the grant was also made by other state officials such as the prince, diwan and nawab.
73. Allahabad Doc. Nos. 3, 32, 47, 165, 166, 175, 760, 814 and 843.
74. Ibid., Nos. 6, 166, 171, 172 and 174.
75. Ibid., Nos. 11, 53, 55. Here it may be pointed out that Aurangzeb in his said farman had specified the sequence of the persons who could claim to be heirs of the deceased grantee i.e. after him or her the grant was to be renewed in favour of the son, daughter or relations. If a grantee had no relations his grant was to be treated as imperial property. K.P. Srivastava, *Mughal Farmans*, Doc. No. 42.
76. Allahabad Doc. Nos. 11, 32, 761, 1189. Allahabad Doc. No. 32 indicates that there were twenty-four heirs of Faizullah in 1715–16 in pargana Daryabad, sarkar Awadh. All of these heirs were given shares after the death of Faizullah.
77. Allahabad Doc. No. 1236.
78. For instance in 1715 in pargana Darybad, sarkar Awadh, twenty-four heirs of Faizullah applied for the renewal of the grant in their favours. The whole grant of 1,886 *bighas* was divided among them. The division of the grant indicates that the share of each claimant varied from grantee to grantee. Only three heirs got more than 200 *bighas*. Three of them got only 15 *bighas*. Allahabad Doc. No. 32. There are many other references regarding the creation of small *madad-i-maash* holdings due to the division of grants among heirs of deceased grantees (ibid., Nos. 760, 761 and 843).
79. Ibid., 857, 1189.
80. Allahabad Doc. Nos. 44 and 46.
81. Ibid., Nos. 782, 1201 and 1203.
82. Iqbal Husain, '*Madad-i-Maash* Regulation in the Mughal Empire', PIHC, 1977, p. 302.
83. The parwana has been translated by Shaikh Abdur Rashid in the *Journal of the Pakistan Historical Society*, vol. IX, pt. II, pp. 103–4.
84. With the heirs.
85. A *madad-i-maash* document issued in 1694 records that originally Sayyid Habib was assigned 2,000 *bighas* of *madad-i-maash* lands in pargana Bhagalpur, sarkar

Monghyr, suba Bihar. After his death one half of the grant was resumed and the other half was confirmed to his son Sayyid Mir Iqbal Husain. '*Madad-i-Maash* Regulation', PIHC, 1977, p. 308. Another document indicates that the grant of the Jogis of Jakhbar in suba Lahore was resumed during Aurangzeb's reign. J.S. Grewal and B.N. Goswamy, *The Mughals and Jogis of Jakhbar*, pp. 126–30.

86. Allahabad Doc. Nos. 3, 7, 760, 765, 796, 812, 822, 830, 831, 848; NAI, 1740, 1831, 2162, 2578/13.
87. Iqbal Husain, '*Madad-i-Maash* Regulation', PIHC, 1977, p. 304.
88. Muzaffar Alam, *The Crisis of Empire*, p. 220.
89. NAI, 1651.
90. Ibid., 1273, 1434.
91. For example, Qazi Imad-ud-Din was assigned 500 bighas of *madad-i-maash* lands in pargana Sandila, sarkar Lucknow in 1677. NAI, 1360. In the same year he was assinged the duty to construct a well and to layout a garden. He therefore was assigned 10 *bighas* of *madad-i-maash* lands in pargana Sandila, sarkar Lucknow. Ibid., 1393. In 1678–9 he received villages (*manzas*) Mambi and Kori as *madad-i-maash* grant to meet the expenses of the *khanqah*. Ibid. In 1679 he was given Rs. 200 and 250 as *madad-i-maash* grant in addition to the lands already assigned. Ibid., 1374.
92. In 1667 the *madad-i-maash* grant of 500 *bighas* of Shaikh Izzadullah was transferred from one place to another because of strained relations between him and the people of that place. Allahabad Doc. Nos. 1190–1, 1192. In 1697 the grant of Shaikh Abdul Faiz was transferred to another area due to the hostility of the local people. Ibid., 1212.
93. In 1681, Ishaq and Muhammad made mutual transfer of their *madad-i-maash* lands, Allahabad Doc. No. 274.
94. Allahabad Doc. Nos. 782, 1203. Compare Irfan Habib, *Agrarian System of Mughal India*, Bombay, 1963, p. 300.
95. Allahabad Doc. No. 1203.
96 Ibid., 1189. Compare Irfan Habib, *Agrarian System*, p. 304.
97. Allahabad Doc. Nos. 11, 53 and 54.
98. In the sixteenth century Abdul Quddus Gangohi, a theologist declared *ushr* an illegal tax imposed on the *khudkashta* of the grantees. He made a plea to the state not to impose *ushr* on grantees. In late sixteenth century Jalal-ud-Din Thaneswari, student of Abdul Quddus Gangohi made a plea for all grants held by Muslims to be treated as their property (*milk*) with the condition on the owners to pay *ushr*. Zafar-ul-Islam, 'Nature of Landed Property in Mughal India: Views of an 18th Century Jurist', PIHC, 1975, pp. 301–9. Although the plea made by Gangohi and Thaneswari to legitimize the *milkiyat* rights of *aimadars* over their *madad-i-maash* land was not considered by the state, but the rights exercised by the grantees assert that they were practical properietors of their assigned lands.
99. Allahabad Doc. No. 1196.
100. Ibid., Nos. 1216, 1219, 1221, 1222 and 1224.
101. Ibid., Nos. 892, 1230 and 1231.

CHAPTER 4

Concentration and Dispersal

The concentration and dispersal of *madad-i-maash* grant in the particular region during the Mughal period was based on socio-political considerations. The *madad-i-maash* grants were given for charitable purposes. But the size of holdings, and the families selected for assignments, indicate that the objective was also to create a class which could watch the interests of the state at the local level and pray for the state. The creation of *madad-i-maash* holders as a class was, therefore, not simply an act of charity. But it was a group that promoted the interests of the state.[1] To quote Irfan Habib. 'The state had its own interest in maintaining this class (*madad-i-maash* holder). Jahangir called it the army of prayer. . . . The grantees were its creatures and therefore, its natural apologist and propagandists.' The creation of *madad-i-maash* holders as a class was, therefore, not simply an act of charity. But it was a group that promoted the interests of the state.

What were the factors responsible for the concentration dispersal of these grants in a region?

THE AREAS OF CONCENTRATION

The assignment of revenue as *madad-i-maash* formed a small portion of the total *jama* (revenue) of a suba. It is difficult to specify the total area of *madad-i-maash* lands in the absence of the statistics of such grants in our period. However, the *sayurghal* figures in the *Ain-i-Akbari* indicate that 4.31 per cent revenue of the total *jama* of the suba of Awadh was assigned as *madad-i-maash* grants.[2] All five sarkars of Awadh had some area of *madad-i-maash* lands. In the sarkars Awadh, Gorakhpur, Bahraich, Khairabad and Lucknow, 4.1 per cent, 0.42 per cent, 1.93 per cent, 0.39 per cent and 5.65 per cent of the total *jama* was assigned as *madad-i-maash* respectively.[3] Similarly the percentage of such grants at pargana level also varied. In the suba, in 82 out of 133 parganas, some parts of the total *jama* were *madad-i-maash* grants,[4] whereas in 52 parganas no portion of the total *jama* was granted as *madad-i-maash*.[5]

It seems that *madad-i-maash* was assigned in different parganas according to local conditions.[6]

The highest percentage of *madad-i-maash* was 23.3 in pargana Ibrahimabad, sarkar Awadh. In Sarkar Gorakhpur no pargana consisted more than 2 per cent of total *jama*.[7] In sarkar Bahraich, only pargana Haveli Bahraich had 4.4 per cent *madad-i-maash* lands of the total *jama* and other parganas covered below than 5 per cent. In sarkar Khairabad, parganas Gopamau and Hargaraon *madad-i-maash* occupied 10 per cent and 13 per cent of total *jama* respectively and most of the remaining parganas, except Khairabad, Sandi and Laharpur, had the area of *madad-i-maash* less than 3 per cent of the *jama*.[9] In sarkar Lucknow the revenue assigned as *madad-i-maash* was higher than in other sarkars.[10]

The percentage figures show that *madad-i-maash* was not a heavy burden on the imperial treasury, that the area of such grants was low. *Jama* figures of the *Ain-i-Akbari* indicate only the areas of cultivated land, whereas land assigned as *madad-i-maash* was both cultivated and cultivable. However, such grants were given increasingly in waste but cultivable tracts. This is evident from the fact that a large number of the *madad-i-maash* documents bear the term *zamin-i-uftada, laiq-i-ziriat*, or waste but cultivable lands.[11] Thus it can be assumed that through this practice the state brought gradually cultivable waste land under cultivation. It is, however, difficult to give exact areas of *madad-i-maash* lands in the suba due to lack of statistics.

In the seventeenth century *madad-i-maash* lands were assigned in some parganas of the suba, which have been mentioned as *non-aimma* areas in *Ain-i-Akbari*.[12] Some other references show that in this and the eighteenth century a few new families of the suba emerged as *madad-i-maash* holders. In 1695 Musammat Dulari was assigned villages Korsanda and Malabir[13] in pargana Gopamau, sarkar Khairabad as *madad-i-maash* lands. Earlier these villages had been assigned in *jagir* to Shaikh Muhammad Anwar, the son of Mst. Dulari.[14] The instances of the assignment of *madad-i-maash* lands in new areas and the emergence of new *madad-i-maash* holders families suggests that the extent of *madad-i-maash* grants in the suba was now larger than in Akbar's time. Here it may be clarified that from Aurangzeb's reign onwards there is hardly any example of cancellation of *madad-i-maash* grant to a family of Awadh. In fact, the families increased the area of their *madad-i-maash* lands.[15]

Regarding the concentration and distribution of high and low percentages of *madad-i-maash* grants in different areas, two opinions have been experessed. First, 'there was a tendency to favour localities with Muslim zamindars for sites of land grants in comparison with those with non-Muslim zamindars'.[16] Second, 'the class of grant holders was town based and their areas of grants concentrated in the tracts with larger population'.[17] However, these opinions need reconsideration. As far as the first view is concerned it is true in relation to some parganas of Awadh. There were 11 parganas of the suba in Akbar's reign which had Muslim zamindars. Of these, 4 covered more than 10 per cent of the revenue of their *jama* as *madad-i-maash.*[18] The other 4 parganas comprised above 5 per cent while in the remaining 2, the proportion was lower.[19] The total *madad-i-maash* lands of parganas with Muslim zamindars were 8.762 of gross *jama* and with non-Muslim zamindars these were 3.70 per cent. Thus the total average of *madad-i-maash* grants of the parganas with Muslim zamindars was higher than the parganas with non-Muslim zamindars.[20] However, the above hypothesis is not applicable as a general rule regarding the concentration and distribution of *madad-i-maash* grants in all parganas of the suba. In Awadh the parganas where Muslim zamindars settled were few in number.[21] Only 12.94 per cent of the total parganas of Awadh with *madad-i-maash* grants had Muslim zamindars. The rest had non-Muslim zamindars. A number of such parganas were assigned a considerable part of *jama* as *madad-i-maash* grants. In 3 of these parganas, more than 10 per cent of the *jama* was *madad-i-maash*[22] while 14 parganas had more than 5 per cent.[23]

The variations in the concentration of high and low percentage of *madad-i-maash* assignment seems to have been based on local conditions. In the sarkars Awadh and Lucknow the percentage of *madad-i-maash* was relatively high with many parganas showing a higher percentage of *madad-i-maash* assignment.[24] On the contrary the sarkars Gorakhpur, Bahraich and Khairabad had low percentages of *madad-i-maash* lands. Even in these sarkars the parganas with Muslim zamindars covered small parts of the areas as grants. Pargana Utraula in the sarkar of Gorakhpur, with Muslim zamindars, had only 0.5 per cent *madad-i-maash* lands.[25] A plausible reason for such variation is the fertility of the land.

This hypothesis can be tested on the basis of the sizes of the grant holdings of some families in five sarkars. The available documents show that there was great similarity in the sizes of *madad-i-maash* holdings of these five sarkars. In every sarkar small and large size of holdings were assigned to the *madad-i-maash* holders.[26] In view of the varied fertility of the assigned land the yield from the same was not necessarily in accordance with the area of fertile land. Thus the higher and lower percentages of *madad-i-maash* grants in different sarkars varied on the basis of fertility of soil.

Concerning the concentration of *madad-i-maash* grants in those areas which had larger urban populaitons, we can on the basis of archaeological remains explore the locations of towns[27] and trace the areas with marketing centres. The available evidence from Awadh shows that the sarkars of Lucknow, Awadh and Khairabad had a number of monuments and in these areas the concentration of *madad-i-maash* grants was relatively.[28] The sarkars Bahraich and Gorakhpur had low concentrations of grants and these areas also have only a few monuments.[29] This can be further confirmed by another method of tracing the areas of marketing centres. The *District Gazetteers* and *Settlement Reports* of the United Provinces also mention that the areas showing concentration of *madad-i-maash* grants had *dargahas* (shrines) of local Sufi saints.

In most of the areas of the suba, the descendants of Sayyid Salar Masud[30] and Sufi Sayyid Ashraf Jahangir[31] were settled.[32] Since these two saints were famous their descendants received considerable respect from the local people. From the thirteenth centruy onwards the shrines of Sufis and their living descendants received land grants from the imperial authority for the maintenance of the *dargahs.* The *dargahs* were not only places of pilgrimage but it was customary to organize *urs* and fairs in the memory of Sufis.[33] Such functions also served the marketing purposes of the local people. They helped

TABLE 1: SOME SUFI SHRINES OF AWADH

S. No.	*Pargana*	*Dargahs*
1	Pargana Haveli Awadh	6[34]
2	Maghar	1[35]
3	Bangarmau	1[36]
4	Dewa	Many[37]
5	Rudauli	1[38]
6	Satrikh	1[39]
7	Kakori	5[40]
8	Bahraich	1[41]
9	Mallawan	2[42]
10	Sandila	1[43]
11	Gopamau	1[44]
12	Pargana Haveli Khairabad	1[45]

develop commercial life in neighbouring areas. It is important that in Awadh almost every pargana had a Sufi shrine and Table 1 shows the existence of *dargahs* in some parganas of suba Awadh.

Besides the above, there were numerous other *dargahs* in different pargans of the suba.[46]

Apart from *dargahs* there were number of *khanqahs* and *sarais.*[47] These provided food and shelter to the needy and to travellers. More importantly the *khanqahs* also extended help to students. The *khanqah* and *sarais* helped the growth of urban life in the Mughal period.

The existence of monuments, *dargahs*, *khanqahs* and *sarais* indicate that *madad-i-maash* were concentrated in urban areas. However, it does not mean that the concentration of *madad-i-maash* lands was solely town based. The concentration of *madad-i-maash* lands in areas with larger urban populations was limitd to conditional grant holders such as *qazis*, *sajjada nashins* and *mutawallis.* But there were number of unconditional grantees, who had a rural base. Though these grantees had relatively small holdings, at the local level they had considerable influence among the people and were larger in number than the grantees of urban areas.

It is evident from *madad-i-maash* documents that some grantees had their residence in the villages where they had been assigned *madad-i-maash* lands.[48] More importantly the grantees were instructed by the state to live in those villages.[49] Moreover, the grantees who had small holdings in waste land[50] had no other means of livelihood except the assigned land. It was difficult for them to depend on tenants for cultivation. As they were not wealthy they had to make the land fertile themselves. They could not afford to have live in the towns. They were therefore compelled to settle in rural areas. Moreover the grant holders who had both cultivated and waste cultivable lands, were instructed by the state to bring first the waste cultivable lands (*uftada*) under cultivation.[51] Thus the grantees whose holdings were small were village based.

The rural base of *madad-i-maash* grants are further illustrated by the fact that the *qazis* and other officials of the religio-judicial departments were also appointed in the villages.[52] Some records indicate that mosques and *madrasas* were built in rural areas.[53] It may be mentioned that *qazis*, mosques and *madrasas* were regular assignees of *madad-i-maash* lands, therefore, it can be assumed that the *madad-i-maash* lands to the above institutions were concentrated in rural areas.

The increasing power of *madad-i-maash* holders in terms of acquisition of *zamindari* rights led to conflict with other zamindars of the area.[54] It was their economic interests that clashed. Agrarian surplus was the main source of the income of both zamindars and *madad-i-maash* holders, and to expropriate it they came into direct conflict.[55] This suggests that the grantees who challenged the authority of the local zamindars had a large number of followers in the villages and had themselves settled in the same areas.

Above all, since the state had its own interest in the creation of *madad-i-maash* holders as a class it is wrong to assert that the creation of this class was limited to towns. In the suba of Awadh, rural areas were more disturbed than the urban. The zamindars of the large parts of the suba had become defiant. It was hardly expected from them that they would be helpful in establishing social and political harmony in their regions. Consequently *madad-i-maash* holders were used as a effective means to mobilize people of villages in favour of state, which was more interested in concentrating *madad-i-maash* grants in rural areas.

Madad-i-maash grants were concentrated in certain selected villages in each pargana, distinct from the villages of *khalsa* and *jagir* lands. True, some references have been also found that *madad-i-maash* lands were given in *jagir* and *khalsa* lands.[56] Such lands assigned in *jagir* and *khalsa* were divided into two categories; peasant held (*raiyati*) and self-cultivated (*khudkashta*). In case of the first, the grantee was assigned only the revenue of the grant lands. The *milikiyat* right of the lands was retained by the peasants.[57] However, the assignment of *madad-i-maash* lands in *jagir* and *khalsa* was nominal, the bulk of the grants being concentrated in the areas embarked as *aimma* villages in each pargana.[58] In such villages *madad-i-maash* grants contained mostly waste cultivable lands (*uftada laiq-i-zirait*) and these were excluded from *jama*. Since waste lands were converted into cultivated lands by the grantees, these were categorized as self-cultivated lands. On such types of lands the grantees had proprietary rights. Such holdings existed on a larger scale than *raiyati*.

The fertility of *madad-i-maash* land varied from area to area and so too the yields. As such it is difficult to trace the exact fertility of the grant lands. The bulk of them were fallow land, whose revenue was not estimated by the Mughal government.

The areas assigned as *madad-i-maash* lands in a particular village are normally mentioned in the documents.[59] In view of varied fertility of lands within a region it is difficult to work out the exact quantum of production under a particular grant. However, on the basis of the available evidences it can be assumed that lands granted as *madad-i-maash* was suitable for productions to meet the needs of the assignees. The *madad-i-maash* lands were not cultivated because they had not been assigned earlier to anyone. The soils of these lands were as good as the soil of cultivated lands. Abul Fazl mentions that the revenue derived from each *bigha* of *madad-i-maash* lands varied but was never less than one rupee.[60] The fertility of the assigned waste cultivable land as *madad-i-maash* was the main consideration, because he had no other means of livelihood. In case the assigned land was unproductive subsistence provided was useless. Being economically weak the grantees were incapable of investing much on the assigned land for the croppings.[61] Therefore, we know of few complaints about the infertility of the land assigned.

Our analysis of the concentration of the areas of *madad-i-maash* grants indicate, first, that they were largely made in the non-revenue yielding areas. It seems the objective was to save the revenue-yielding area for the assignments of jagirs. Since *madad-i-maash* holders were an important class, the state was interested to help them and also provide a mechanism through which waste land may be cultivated. Thus, by this practice the state fulfilled two purposes: it succeeded in extending the areas of cultivation and more importantly it received the goodwill of a religious class that was quite influential.

Second, the concentration of high and low percentages of the cultivated areas or revenue-yielding lands varied from sarkar to sarkar. The locations of the assignments as *madad-i-maash* were determined irrespective of the religion of the local zamindars. Though the size of the cultivated area assigned in *madad-i-maash* in Muslim-dominated *zamindari* was higher, the number of Muslim zamindars in parganas of the suba were less. Moreover, it may be pointed out that of five sarkars of the suba the Muslim zamindars were only in a few parganas of two sarkars. However, in these two sarkars the percentage of *madad-i-maash* grant was relatively higher. Even in them, some parganas with non-Muslim zamindars had a higher percentage of land in *madad-i-maash*. Thus it can be assumed that high and low percentages of revenue-yielding areas assigned as *madad-i-maash* grants varied due to considerations other than the composition of the local zamindars.

Third, *madad-i-maash* lands was both urban and rural based. In the urban areas the *madad-i-maash* were assigned to important families concerned with religious and judicial departments. But the importance of the rural *madad-i-maash* holders cannot be under estimated, because these families held important positions at the loca level.

Fourth, the grant was concentrated in certain areas as assignments from *khalsa* and *jagir* lands was avoided. Though few references are available regarding the assignment of *madad-i-maash* lands in *jagir* areas, during our period the bulk of grants were concentrated in the areas embarked as *aimma* lands.

SOME IMPORTANT FAMILIES OF *MADAD-I-MAASH* HOLDERS IN THE SUBA

The *madad-i-maash* grants during the Mughal period was distributed among the families who were not rich, religiously known, and socially influential. This categorization holds irrespective of clan and community. However, the bulk of *madad-i-maash* holders of Awadh belonged to learned men and men of noble lineage.

It has been postulated that the *madad-i-maash* grant was only meant for the Muslims in Mughal India[62] but available references indicate that its benefit was extended to the non-Muslim families also. From Akbar's reign to the eighteenth century, non-Muslim *madad-i-maash* holders enjoyed grants in the same way as did Muslim familes.[63]

In 1672–3 Aurangzeb issued a general order for the resumption of the grants of non-Muslims. But the available references regarding the confirmations of such grants in that period indicate that this order was not implemented.[64] There is hardly any reference to the confiscation of *madad-i-maash* grants of non-Muslims in the light of this order. More significantly, there was no opposition from non-Muslim grantees to this order. Thus it seems that the order was not issued to harass non-Muslim grantees. After 1670 the empire was facing a political crisis. Many Hindu chiefs had revolted against Aurangzeb. Perhaps Aurangzeb, in a moment of anger, thought to punish Hindus by issuing this order, but practically it was not enforced. Even after 1679 Aurangzeb continued to confirm *madad-i-maash* grants to Hindu assignees. It is believed that after that year Aurangzeb adopted an anti-Hindu policy for the reimposition of *jazia*. But this hypothesis also seems to be unfounded in the context of *madad-i-maash* grants made to Hindu in 1679 and later.[65]

However, the fact remains that in the suba Awadh there were a few non-Muslim grantees. The family of Lal Missir was granted 200 *bighas* of lands during Jahangir's reign in pargana Laharpur, sarkar Lucknow. In the subsequent period Aurangzeb did not confiscate the grant and the family continued to hold that position and received another grant in pargana Sandila, sarkar Lucknow.[66] The family of Harcharan was assigned *madad-i-maash* lands in pargana Haveli Awadh of Nawab Shauja-ud-Daula.[67]

There was no specific practice of proportional distribution of *madad-i-maash* grants between Muslim and non-Muslim families in a particular area. Thus it is wrong to assert that there was any religious reason behind the relatively small-scale distribution of grants to the families of Hindu. The plausible reasons can be seen in the light of the segments of Hindu society. There was a general feeling in Hindu society that donations from the state and individuals could be received only by Brahmans. Since a selection of the Brahmans of medieval India were reasonably prosperous, it seems that they did not need financial help. By performance rituals the Brahmans collected wealth. The Hindu temples and other religious institutions were aided by the Hindu zamindars and chiefs. Moreover, it was a general practice among Hindus that whenever one went to the temple he donated something to it. All these practices were sources of the income for Brahman. And if any needy Brahman applied for the grant he was not deprived of the same.

Like Muslim grantees, non-Muslims were also expected to pray for the betterment of the everlasting empire.[68] They were understood to be active in the 'army of prayers'.[69] Thus it can be inferred that though non-Muslim grantees were in a minority, they occupied the same status as Muslim grantees as regards to the objectives of such grants.

The majority of *madad-i-maash* holders of Awadh belonged to the Shaikh and Sayyid families, believed to be descendants of Prophet and a pious class.[70] However, the families of *madad-i-maash* holder can be categorized into four sections: the families of *qazis, mutawallis, muftis* and other officials of religio-judicial departments; *sajjda nashins*, those who controlled educational and religious institutions; and those who were assigned *madad-i-maash* lands for their maintenance and did not render any service to the state.

THE *QAZIS*—SOME IMPORTANT FAMILIES

In Awadh the families of the *qazis* appropriated a considerable part of grant lands. They were assigned two types of *madad-i-maash* grants, land in lieu of services rendered as *qazis*.[71] and land for public welfare purposes.[72] Some *qazis* were also given daily and annual allowance as *madad-i-maash* grants.[73]

There were many families of *qazis* who enjoyed a significant place in the socio-economic and political life of the suba. Genealogical and other details of a few families are available and given below.

(i) *Family of Qazi Imad-ud-Din*

The family of Qazi Imad-ud-Din of pargana Sandila, sarkar Lucknow, was one of the prominent families of the suba. References are found to the familie's *madad-i-maaash* lands and post of *qazi* prior to Shahjahan's reign. A document shows that Qazi Abdul Halim of this family succeeded his father Abdur Rauf in 1632.[74] During Aurangzeb's reign, Abdul Hakim was succeeded by his son Mubarak.[75] In 1671 Imad-ud-Din succeeded his father, Qazi Mubarak. At this time Imad-ud-Din was given *madad-i-maash* of Rs. 250, with Rs. 203 as annual allowances.[76] In 1673 he received Rs. 300 to meet the expenses of his kinsmen.[77] In 1677 he was confirmed as *qazi* of pargana Sandila, sarkar Lucknow.[78] In 1680 he was appointed as *muhatasib*[79] and *nirkh navis*[80] of pargana Sandila.[81] Besides these duties, Imad-ud-Din was also assigned *madad-i-maash* lands of great importance. In 1677, 500 *bighas madad-i-maash* land were confirmed in his favour in lieu of salary.[82] In the same year he was assigned 10 *bighas* in village Mathsova, pargana Sandila, sarkar Lucknow for laying out a garden.[83] In 1678 he was given *madad-i-maash* lands in villages Mambi and Kori to meet the expenses of a *khanqah*.[84] He was assigned number of other *madad-i-maash* holdings which testify to a certain level of prosperity.[85] In 1700 Qazi Imad-ud-Din was succeeded by his son Sharaf-ud-Din.[86] In 1702 Sharaf-ud-Din was confirmed as *qazi* of pargana Sandila.[87] He was assigned *madad-i-maash* lands in lieu of his services.[88] He was succeed by his son, Qazi Zakaria.[89] The family retained the post of *qazi* and its *madad-i-maash* lands through the century.[90]

(ii) *Family of Qazi Abdul Ghafur*

The family of Qazi Abdul Ghafur of pargana Gopamau sarkar, Khairabad was another important *madad-i-maash* holder family of the suba. It had occupied the post of *qazi* for a long period. Rahimullah, the founder of this family, came to India from Central Asia with Taimur in the fourteenth century. At that time he was appointed governor of Kashmir. In the sixteenth century, the family of Rahimullah migrated to Awadh and settled in pargana Gopamau.[91] The family held the post of *qazi* during Humayun's reign.[92] During Shah Jahan's reign Abdul

Hamid of this family was appointed *qazi* and assigned 261 *bighas* and 4 *bighas* of *madad-i-maash* lands. He was succeeded by Abdul Ghafur.[93] The family retained the *qaziship* of the pargana Gopamau until the time of the annexation of Awadh.[94]

(iii) *The Family of Qazi Muhammad*

The family of Muhammad of pargana and sarkar Khairabad also retained the post of *qazi* for a long time. This family was engaged in religious duties prior to Akbar's reign. During Akbar's reign it came into prominence and Shaikh Muhammad was appointed *imam*, *muhatasib*, *mutawalli* and *qazi* of pargana Khairabad and was assigned *madad-i-maash* lands.[95] He was succeeded by Raje.[96] In 1579, Shaikh Ahmad, son of Raje, was assigned 250 *bighas madad-i-maash* lands in village Karanpur, pargana Khairabad.[97] Raje was succeeded by Qazi Muhammad Hasan.[98] In 1658 Daim succeeded Muhammad Hasan and he was assigned 5 *bighas* of *madad-i-maash* lands for the construction of a mosque, *khanqah* and a *madrasa*.[99] This family retained the post until the nineteenth century.[100] It is important to note that the successors of Daim assumed *zamindari* rights in pargana Khairabad on the basis of *madad-i-maash* lands, granted to him.[101] In the middle of the nineteenth century, Amin-ud-Din, one of the successors of Daim, sought the legitimacy of his *zamindari* rights in kasba Panwaria, pargana Khairabad. Subsequently, it was testified by 30 per cent of the people of the kasba that Amin-ud-Din had hereditary *zamindari* rights over qasba Panwaria.[102]

SAJJADA NASHINS

There were numerous *dargahs* (shrines) of local Sufis in the suba of Awadh.[103] It was a common belief in medieval India that a Sufi burial in a shrine has supernatural powers. Such shrines were protected by the state. The descendants of deceased Sufis were assigned *madad-i-maash* lands for the maintenance of the shrines and *khanqahs*.[104] The controller of shrine and *khanqah* was called *sajjada nashin* or *pirzada*.[105]

From the Sultanate period the *sajjada nashins* of Awadh were given revenue free lands.[106] During the Mughal period they received considerable political patronage. An inscription of the first half of the eighteenth century in the *dargah* of Sayyid Salar Masud of Bahraich indicates that six villages were assigned for its maintenance.[107]

During the period under study many families of *sajjada nashin* in Awadh, were given sizeable lands as *madad-i-maash*. But it is difficult to give genealogical details of these families, because references to them are not available in a systematic way. However, as *madad-i-maash* grants were declared hereditary rights, these families retained the grants generation after generation.[108] The families of Qazi Habibullah,[109] and Imad-ud-Din,[110] Shaikh Izzatullah,[111] Karamullah,[112] and Amanullah,[113] Sayyid Muhammad Baqa[114] and Muhammad Wafa Ashrafi[115] were the prominent *sajjada nashin madad-i-maash* holders of the suba.

THE FAMILIES AND EDUCATIONAL AND RELIGIOUS INSTITUTIONS

In medieval India persons of the *ulema* class were engaged in the development of education that was generally based on religion and centred in religious buildings. Mosques, *khanqahs*, *maths* and temples were also used for educational purposes. Medieval Indian states provided necessary help in terms of *madad-i-maash* grants for the maintenance of these institutions. The families who ran them were also given *madad-i-maash* lands for their own maintenance. Even students received financial help from the *khanqah*.[116] The *madad-i-maash* grants to the teachers helped them promote education in their areas.

Educationally, Awadh was one of the most developed subas of Mughal India. The families who controlled the educational institutions enjoyed considerable areas of *madad-i-maash* lands. The scholars of pargana Bilgram, sarkar Lucknow were famous all over the country.

The most prominent *madad-i-maash* holder family engaged in education in the suba was the family of Mulla Qutub-ud-Din of pargana Sihali, sarkar Lucknow.[117] Qutub-ud-Din, a learned person of Aurangzeb's reign, belonged to the family which had an established reputation in academic pursuits.The ancestors of Mulla Qutub-ud-Din belonged to Horat.[118] The period of the migration of the family from Horat to India is unknown, but biographies of the family mention that Mukhdum Alauddin settled in Sihali in the beginning of the fourteenth century.[119] Mulla Hafiz, the grandfather of Qutub-ud-Din, was granted 2,600 *bighas* of *madad-i-maash* lands in pargana Fatehpur, sarkar Lucknow by Emperor Akbar in 1559.[120]

During Aurangzeb's reign Mulla Qutub-ud-Din, the grandson of Mulla Hafiz, ran a *madrasa* at Sihali.[121] He retained the *madad-i-maash* grants of his ancestors. He had many disciples from different parts of the country.[122] In 1690 Mulla Qutub-ud-Din was killed by the khanzada zamindars of Sihali[123] and the family migrated to Lucknow. The family was given Firangi Mahal by Emperor Aurangzeb, where Mulla Nizam-ud-Din, son of Mulla Qutub-ud-Din,[124] established a *madrasa* and was granted 112 *bighas madad-i-maash* lands in pargana Dewa, sarkar Lucknow in addition to an earlier grant. Bahadur Shah I granted a daily stipend of two rupees to Mulla Nizam-ud-Din. These grants were enjoyed by the family throughout eighteenth century.[125]

There were many other families who managed the *maktab, madrasa* and mosque. Some families were also given *madad-i-maash* land for the construction of mosques and for the maintenance of their *imams* and *muazzin*.[126] But the genealogy of these families are not available and it is difficult to give their history. However, in the suba most of the towns and villages had mosques, used for prayer and educational purposes, and *madad-i-maash* lands were assigned to those who managed them.

THE FAMILIES WHICH HELD UNCONDITIONAL GRANTS

There were several families in the suba who were assigned *madad-i-maash* lands without any obligation. Such grantees were either members of influential families or poor. Such assignees were in the majority. The documents issued to these families record that they had no other means of livelihood.[127] However, the sizes of the holdings of *madad-i-maash* lands of some grantees indicate that the grants were not only intended to help the grantees to earn their livelihood, but the objective behind them was to extend considerable financial support so that they could maintain a respectable position in society. In 1695 Mst. Dulari was granted two villages yielding a revenue of Rs. 15,269 as *madad-i-maash* in pargana Gopamau, sarkar Khairabad for the maintenance of her family.[128] It deserves to be mentioned that the son of Mst. Dulari was jagirdar. In 1695 he died and his family had nothing for its maintenance. It is significant that the jagir of her son was converted into *madad-i-maash* lands in her favour.[129] In sarkar Gorakhpur, many women grantees were assigned 200 *bighas* and above[130] for the same purpose. Most of the women grantees were widows.

Muhammad Arif, a *madad-i-maash* holder during Aurangzeb's reign was a prominent person of sarkar Bahraich. The original *madad-i-maash* was assigned to his ancestor Sayyid Masud in Jahangir's reign.

In Aurangzeb's reign Muhammad Arif declared himself the heir of Sayyid Masud and received his *madad-i-maash* lands. In 1663 357 *bighas* and 12 *biswas* was confirmed as *madad-i-maash* lands[131] in his favour. Sayyid Muhammad Arif received greater favour from the state than his predecessors. Not only was the whole grant of his ancestors confirmed but he was also assigned *madad-i-maash* lands in three parganas, Bahraich, Hisampur and Fakhrpur.[132] It may be pointed out that normally *madad-i-maash* land was granted only in one pargana to a particular grantee. Having a sizeable grant under his control, Muhammad Arif established an respectable position in his area. Subsequently he purchased *zamindari* rights in many villages in pargana Hisampur, sarkar Bahraich.[133] Even on his *madad-i-maash* lands he excercised *zamindari* rights. In 1698 he leased out his *madad-i-maash* lands in pargana Haveli Bahraich.[134] In 1704 Muhammad Arif was succeeded by his son Muhammad Naqi[135] and the family retained the grant through the rest of the century.

Besides the above-mentioned *madad-i-maash* holder families, there were many whose grant holdings were quite small. It seems that the distribution of *madad-i-maash* grants in terms of size of the holdings varied from family to family and dependend on the nature of work and the social influence of allottee. *Qazis*, *sajjada nashins* and controllers of educational and religious institutions were assigned sizeable lands because they had greater responsibilities than other types of the grantees. Others were given relatively small holdings because the grants were used by them only for their own maintenance. The unconditional grant holder family such as the family of Muhammad Arif of paragana and sarkar Bahraich was favoured with large *madad-i-maash* grants because of his local influence. However, the *madad-i-maash* grants in the suba were generally distributed among families of aristocratic descent, such as Shaikhs, Sayyids and Brahmans.

NOTES

1. Irfan Habib, *Agrarian System of Mughal India*, Bombay, 1963 p. 310.
2. Shireen Moosvi, '*Sayurghal* Statistics in the *Ain-i-Akbari*, An Analysis', *Indian Historical Review*, 1976, p. 286. *Ain-i-Akbari*, vol. II, translated by Jarret, mentions 4.2 per cent *madad-i-maash* grants in Awadh of total *jama*, p. 183.
3. *Ain.*, vol. II (English trans.), pp. 184–90.
4. Ibid.

5. The areas embarked as *madad-i-maash* lands varied sarkar to sarkar. In the sarkar of Awadh 2 parganas, Anhonah and Bilhari, had no *madad-i-maash* lands. In sarkar of Gorakhpur 18 out of 24 parganas had no grant lands. In sarkar Bahraich 6 out of 11 parganas had no *madad-i-maash* lands. Sarkar Khairabad had no grant lands in 7 out of 22 parganas. In 18 out of 55 parganas of sarkar Lucknow, the areas of *madad-i-maash* land were nil. Ibid.
6. In sarkar Awadh, 7 parganas occupied more than 5 per cent *madad-i-maash* land of the total *jama.* Appendix A.
7. Appendix A.
8. Ibid.
9. Ibid.
10. Ibid.
11. According to B.R. Grover, 'it is clear from the document that the practice of alienating the greater share (or *madad-i-maash*) from the waste cultivable lands was followed till the eighteenth century', Presidential Address, PIHC, 1976, p. 157. A number of grant documents mention that the area assigned as *madad-i-maash* was demarcated entirely fallow lands. Allahabad Doc. Nos. 8, 156, 157, 158, 160 and 163.
12. In *Ain.*, vol. I, pargana Asoha of sarkar Lucknow is mentioned as non-*aimma* pargana, whenever in seventeenth century there are many references of the assignment of *madad-i-maash* lands in the same pargana. For instance in 1648 Qazi Abdul Shakur was assigned 210 *bighas* as *madad-i-maash* grant in pargana Asoha, sarkar Lucknow. NAI, 2154. In 1654 Bibi Fatima, Qazi Abdul Shakur and Qazi Maudud were assigned 200, 50 and 40 *bighas* respectively as *madad-i-maash* lands in pargana Asoha, sarkar Lucknow, NAI, 2132, 2123, 2140.
13. These villages yielded the revenue of Rs. 15,269 annually. M.A. Ansari, *Administrative Documents,* Doc. No. 28.
14. Ibid., Doc. No. 28.
15. Qazi Imad-ud-Din was assigned quite large areas of *madad-i-maash* land during Aurangzeb's reign in pargana Sandila, sarkar Lucknow. He also got an increase in the area of his assigned land from time to time. NAI, 1360, 1373, 1374 and 1390.
16. Shireen Moosvi, '*Sayurghal* Statistics', *IHR,* 1976, No. 2, p. 283.
17. Ibid., p. 289.
18. Pargana Ibrahimabad in the sarkar of Awadh, the parganas Unnao, Sidhor and Lucknow in the sarkar of Lucknow consisted of 23.30 per cent, 12.60 per cent, 18.49 per cent and 13.80 per cent respectively of the *madad-i-maash* lands of total *jama. Ain.*, vol. II (English trans.), pp. 184–9.
19. The parganas Satanpur and Satrikh in the sarkar of Awadh, Amethi, and Bilgram in the sarkar of Lucknow occupied 6.09 per cent, 8.23 per cent, 6.23 per cent and 6.96 per cent *madad-i-maash* lands respectively of gross *jama. Ain.*, vol. II, pp. 184–9.
20. Shireen Moosvi '*Sayurghal* Statistics', *IHR,* 1976, No. 2, p. 291.
21. The 11 parganas, Ibrahimabad, Satanpur, Satrikh, Utraula, Amethi, Unnao,

Sidhor, Lucknow, Manawi, Saron and Bilgram, had Muslim zamindars. *Ain.*, vol. II (English trans.), pp. 184–9.

22. In the parganas, Hargaon in sarkars Khairabad and Sahali and Mohan in sarkar Lucknow *madad-i-maash* grants constituted 13 per cent, 19 per cent and 10.07 per cent respectively. Ibid., pp. 188–90. Appendix A.
23. The parganas Awadh, Rudauli, Kishni, Mangalsi, Thanah Bhadaon, Khairabad, Zaharpur, Asiyun, Bijnaur, Dewi, Gopamau, Sandila, Fatehpur and Mallawan had *madad-i-maash* grants constituting 7.90 per cent, 8.28 per cent, 9.24 per cent, 6.35 per cent, 8.50 per cent, 8.05 per cent, 6.90 per cent, 7.63 per cent 7.74 per cent, 9 per cent, 7.88 per cent, 8.26 per cent and 6.16 per cent respectively. Ibid., pp. 184–90. Appendix A.
24. Appendix A.
25. The parganas Manawi and Saron with Muslim zamindars in sarkar Lucknow had only 1.77 per cent and 1.45 per cent of *jama* as *madad-i-maash*, Appendix A.
26. The size of holdings varied from grantee to grantee. In all sarkars from 11 to 1,000 *bighas*. Even villages were assigned to the grantees as *madad-i-maash*. Allahabad Doc. Nos. 3, 9, 32, 1345, 1370 and 1409.
27. Shireen Moosvi, '*Sayurghal* Statistics', p. 289.
28. Ibid.
29. Ibid.
30. Sayyid Salar was a general of Mahmud Gaznavi with whom he came to India. He defeated the local chiefs of Bahraich and settled there. His tomb lies in Bahraich. His shrine has a great importance. *Oudh Gazetteer*, vol. I, p. 111.
31. Sayyid Ashraf Jahangir came to India from Iran in the beginning of the fourteenth century. He settled in village Rasulpur, suba Allahabad. He was a celebrated saint of his age. His shrine is constructed at Rasulpur, also known as Kichancha, and Ashrafpur. H.R. Nevill, *Faizabad District Gazetteer*, pp. 237, 259–60.
32. Sharif-ul-Hasan Bilgrami, *Tarikh-i-Khat-i-Pak Bilgram*, Aligarh, 1958, p. 36.
33 Ibid., p. 46.
34. *Oudh Gazetteer*, vol. I, pp. 485–6. First printed in 1877–8, in 3 vols., reprinted in 1985, Delhi.
35. *Gorakhpur District Gazetteer*, Allahabad, 1909, p. 225.
36. *Barabanki District Gazetteer*, Allahabad, 1904, p. 204.
37. Ibid.
38. *Oudh Gazetteer*, vol. I, p. 263.
39. Ibid.
40. *Oudh Gazetteer*, vol. II, p. 285.
41. Ibid., vol. I, p. 90.
42. *D.G. Hardoi* (H.R. Nevill), Lucknow, 1922, p. 219.
43. *Oudh Gazetteer*, vol. I, p. 74.
44. *Hardoi District Gazetteer*, Lucknow, 1923, p. 187.
45. *Sitapur District Gazetteer* (H.R. Nevill), p. 163.
46. NAI, 1272, Allahabad Doc. No. 26.
47. NAI, 1273, 1379, 1398, 1651, 1652 and 2161.

48. Allahabad Doc. No. 292.
49. Ibid., No. 318.
50. Ibid., Nos. 8, 157, 160. In pargana Fakhrpur, sarkar Bahraich some grantees had been assigned the lands of which three-fourth parts were fallow lands. Allahabad Doc. Nos. 161, 162. Such grantees were forced to tilt fallow lands to earn their livelihood.
51. Irfan Habib, *Agrarian System*, p. 303.
52. J.S. Grewal, *Miscellaneous Articles*, Amritsar, 1974, p. 28.
53. Allahabad Doc. No. 1315.
54. In the late seventeenth century the *madad-i-maash* holders of Awadh acquired *zamindari* rights in many places. Ibid. 824, 1189, 1216, 1221, 1224.
55. Allahabad Doc. No. 24.
56. N.A. Siddiqui, *Land Revenue Administration Under the Mughal (1700–1750)* Bombay, 1970, p. 126; S.Z.F. Jafri, 'Two *Madad-i-Maash* Farmans of Awadh', PIHC, 1979. In 1738 Maulvi was assigned 62 *bighas* of cultivated lands from *khalsa* area in village Mahrayana, pargana Sandila, sarkar Lucknow. Zahiruddin Malik, 'Documents of Muhammad Shah's Reign', *Indo-Iranica*, Calcutta, 1973, Nos. 2 and 3, pp. 117–18.
57. If the grantee interfered with the rights of the peasants his grant was transferred to other place. B.R. Grover, PIHC, 1976, p. 157. A document of pargana Haveli Lucknow indicates that Shaikh Izzatullah, a *madad-i-maash* holder had not cordial relations with the *raiyat* consequently his grant was transferred from original place to another. Allahabad Doc. No. 1190.
58. The practice of separating *madad-i-maash* lands from *khalsa* and *jagir* lands was first implemented by Akbar in 1578. Allahabad Doc. No. 24. From that time onwards it became a well established practice to keep excluded *aimma* villages from *khalsa* and *jagir* areas. Allahabad Doc. Nos. 44 and 46.
59. NAI, 1270, 1296, 1393, 1486, 2165. Allahabad Doc. Nos. 863, 1256. NAI document mentions the names of the villages Somb and Mambi were assigned as *madad-i-maash* in pargana Sandila, sarkar Lucknow during Aurangzeb's reign. Since there are no statistics of the revenue of these areas the fertility of these villages is not known. *Ain.*, vol. II, gives the revenue of every pargana, but its figures are not sufficient indication. On the basic of these figures only the general fertility of the whole pargana can be traced. Since the revenue figures of *Ain.* are based on the revenue of only the cultivated area, the general fertility cannot be applied to *madad-i-maash* grant areas: a larger portion of *madad-i-maash* lands occupied waste cultivable areas.
60. *Ain.*, vol. I (English trans.), p. 280.
61. It may be noted that the grantee was not provided assistance for the cultivation of *uftada laiq-i-zirait* lands. He had to make such lands productive at his own expense. On the contrary the grantee was expected to cultivate the *uftada* lands before using lands that were already cultivated.
62. According to W.H. Wilson, '*aimma* was the land which was granted by the Mughal Government to learned and religious persons of Mohammedanism'. *A*

Glossary of Judicial and Revenue Terms of British India, London, 1875. Sir J.N. Sarkar is of the opinion, 'The Mohammadan rulers of India used to make rent free land to holy men and scholars of their own faith,' *Studies in Aurangzeb's Reign*, Calcutta, 1930, p. 246.

63. In the *Journal of the Pakistan Historical Society*, vols. IV, V, VI and VII Jhan Chand has published some articles which show that a number of cash and land grants were asigned to non-Muslim during Aurangzeb's reign. S.M.Hodivala has drawn attention to 200 *bighas* of *madad-i-maash* lands to Mehrji Rana of Navsari, suba Gujarat, during Akbar's reign. The grant continued through Mughal period. *Studies in Parsi History*, Calcutta, 1930, pp. 152, 178. Irfan Habib opines, 'the benefits of the grants were at the same time extended to non-Muslim divines', *Agrarian System*, p. 310. According to Grewal and Goswamy, '. . . though the state of medieval India were not welfare state in the modern sense of that term, the medieval rulers did extend their patronage of individuals and institutions of an act of charity was confined to the co-religionists of the rulers, particularly after the reign of Akbar who in a sense had "Indianized" the institution of *madad-i-maash*'. *The Mughals, Sikh Rulers and Vaishnavas of Pindori*, Simla, 1969, p. 30.
64. In 1673, 260, 20 and 500 *bighas* of *madad-i-maash* grants were confirmed by Aurangzeb's reign to Madan and Khamand Badfrosh, Purusotam, Purustam Giri Sanyasi and Mohan Badfrosh in the parganas Bhojpur, Nanaur and Peeru, suba Bihar. K.K. Dutta, *Some Mughal Farmans, Sanads and Parwanas*, Patna, 1962, pp. 67, 69, 73 and 74. In 1674, 1675, 1676 and 1678 the grants of Pramanand, Lachman Missri, Mohan Badfrosh, Dukhbhanjan, Laxami Narayan and Murlidhar were confirmed to them in parganas Arrah, Dharampur, Bhojpur and Mehsi, suba Bihar, ibid., pp. 67–84.
65. After 1679 *madad-i-maash* grants to many Hindu grantees were confirmed and continued. The grants of Sunder physician, Autam Badfrosh, Jagdev, Balgovind, Sheo Datta Bharati, Garibnath, Bhimpat Dubey were confirmed in the years 1682, 1685, 1688, 1690, 1695 and 1702 respectively in the parganas Mehsi, Peeru, Majhowa, suba Bihar. K.K. Dutta (ed.), *Some Mughal Farmans*, pp. 26–79. In 1688 Aurangzeb granted *madad-i-maash* lands to Hindu *maths* of Marwar. Satish Chandra, 'Some Religious Grants of Aurangzeb to the Maths in the State of Marwar', PIHC, 1970, vol. I, p. 406.
66. Durga Parsad, *Tarikh-i-Sandila*, Lucknow, 1916, p. 20
67. A.L. Srivastava, *First Two Nawabs of Awadh*, Agra, 1954, p. 266.
68. M.A. Ansari, *Administrative Documents*, pp. 17–38.
69. S.A.I. Tirmizi, *Edicts from the Mughal Harum*, Delhi, 1979, p. xxxiii.
70. In Central Asia also the Sayyids were understood as descendants of Prophet Muhammad and were assigned revenue free land. R.N. Frye (ed.), *The Cambridge History of Iran* (in 8 vols.), vol. 4, Cambridge, 1975, p. 153.
71. Irfan Habib, *Agrarian System*, p. 311.
72. NAI, 1269, 1270, 1372, 1373, 1389 and 1393.
73. Ibid., 1444 and 1752.

74. Qazi Abdul Halim also held the post of *muhatasib* and *mutawalli* of pargana Sandila. NAI 1394.
75. Ibid., 1831.
76. Ibid., 1341.
77. Ibid., 1782.
78. Ibid., 1436.
79. *Muhatasib* was an important police office.
80. *Nirkh navis* had to prepare a schedule of rates after ascertaining the prices everyday.
81. NAI, 1273.
82. Ibid., 1360.
83. Ibid., 1393.
84. NAI, 1373 and 2161. The grant to Qazi Imad-ud-Din for the maintenance of *khanqah* indicates that he also acted as *sajjada nashin.*
85. In 1679, Rs. 200 and 250 respectively were given to Qazi Imad-ud-Din in addition to the *madad-i-maash* assigned earlier. NAI, 1374. In 1680 he was given another *madad-i-maash* of 200 *bighas* when he was appointed as *muhatasib* and *nirkh navis.* ibid., 1434. In 1683 he was given Re.1 as daily allowance. In 1684 he was assigned 17 *bighas* of *madad-i-maash* lands to construct a *khanqah,* lay out a garden, and dig a well, ibid., 1651. In 1694 he was granted *madad-i-maash* lands in the villages Khajari and Dhankhewa, pargana Sandila, ibid., 1443.
86. Ibid., 1305.
87. Ibid., 1410.
88. In 1700 and 1701 Qazi Sharaf-ud-Din was granted 100 and 200 *bighas madad-i-maash* lands respectively in pargana Sandila. NAI, 1305 and 1765.
89. Allahabad Doc. No. 31. In 1731 Qazi Ẓakaria was assigned, *madad-i-maash* lands to meet the expenses of travellers and students, NAI, 1652.
90. Qazi Zakaria was succeeded by Qazi Nasir-ud-Din. He was succeeded by Qazi Said-ud-Din. A document of 1780 bears the seal of Qazi Said-ud-Din and another document of 1800 bears his seal. Allahabad Doc. No. 31. NAI, 1352.
91. *Gazetteer of Province of Awadh,* vol. I, p. 579.
92. Ibid., p. 580.
93. Ibid.
94. Ibid., p. 586.
95. Iqbal Husain, 'Calendar of Khariabad Documents, from 16th to 19th century', *Islamic Culture,* 1979, vol. 53, p. 45.
96. The relationship of Qazi Raje with Shaikh Muhammad is not specified. Ibid., p. 45.
97. Ibid., p. 47.
98. Ibid.
99. Ibid., pp. 47–8.
100. Ibid., p. 48.
101. Iqbal Husain, 'Calendar of Khairabad Documents', *Islamic Culture,* vol. 53, p. 48.

102. Ibid.
103. See Chapter 3.
104. *Khanqah* means a house where a Sufi or his descendants live.
105. Richard M. Eaton, 'The Court of Dargah in 17th Century Deccan', *Indian Economic and Social History Review*, 1973, vol. 10, No. 1, p. 51.
106. In the fifteenth century Sikandar Lodi granted revenue free land to one *sajjada nashin* of pargana Mallwan, sarkar Lucknow. H.R. Nevill, *Hardoi District Gazetteer*, p. 225.
107. H.R. Nevill, *Bahraich District Gazetteer*, p. 49. The *dargah* of Sufi in pargana and sarkar Khairabad was given village Lodhpur as a revenue free grant by Akbar. H.R. Nevill, *Sitapur District Gazetteer*, p. 163.
108. Besides *madad-i-mash* grants the *sajjada nashin* succeeded his predecessor on the basis of hereditary successor. Richard M. Eaton, 'The Court and Dargah', *IESHR*, 1973, No. 1, p. 51.
109. In 1664 Qazi Hibullah was granted *madad-i-maash* lands for the maintenance of a *khanqah* in pargana Sandila, sarkar Lucknow. NAI, 1720.
110. The family of Qazi Imad-ud-Din acted as *sajjada nashin* during the seventeenth and eighteeenth centuries. Since this family also held the post of *qazi*, it enjoyed great privileges in the terms of land occupation. NAI, 1272, 1652.
111. In 1663 Shaikh Izzatullah was confirmed the grant in pargana Firozabad, sarkar Baharaich for the maintenance of a *khanqah*. Allahabad Doc. No. 804.
112. In 1717, 233 *bighas* grant lands were confirmed to Shaikh Karamullah for the maintenance of a sufi *khanqah* in pargana Sandila, sarkar Lucknow. NAI, 1050.
113. 100 *bighas madad-i-maash* lands were confirmed to Shaikh Amanullah for the maintenance of a *khanqah* in pargana Sandila, sarkar Lucknow. NAI, 1379.
114. In 1713 Sayyid Muhammad Baqa was granted village Rokha in pargana Sultanpur, sarkar Awadh for the maintenance of the *dargah* and *khanqah* of Sayyid Ashraf Jahangir. Rafat Bilgrami, 'Some Mughal Revenue Grants to the family and Khanqah of Saiyid Ashraf Jahangir', *Medieval India, A Miscellany*, 1972, vol. II, p. 311. It deserves to be mentioned that the shrine of Sayyid Ashraf Jahangir was constructed at Kichhaucha (Ashrafpur) in pargana Bihar, suba Allahabad. H.R. Nevill, *Faizabad District Gazetteer*, pp. 259–60. The grant given pargana Sultanpur, suba Awadh indicates that the descendants of the Sayyid Ashraf Jahangir settled at this place. It also indicates that *madad-i-maash* lands were also given to those places also where shrines were not located.
115. Muhammad Wafa Ashrafi was assigned village Bhagupur in pargana Bisoli, sarkar Lucknow during Farrukhsiyar's reign for the maintenance of shrine of Sayyid Ashraf Jahangir. R. Bilgrami, 'Some Mughal Revenue Grants', *Medieval India, A Miscellany*, vol. II, p. 303.
116. NAI, 1270, 1625. During Farrukhsiyar's reign the whole village Dhaurahar was granted as *madad-i-maash* for the maintenance of the *khanqah* of Sayyid Ashraf Jahangir. R. Bilgrami, 'Some Revenue Grants Documents', *Medieval India, A Miscellany*, 1972, vol. II, p. 303.

117. M.R. Ansari, 'A Very Early Farman of Akbar', PIHC, 1975, p. 353.
118. Ibid., p. 356.
119. Ibid., pp. 356–7.
120. Ibid., p. 354.
121. Ibid., p. 353.
122. Shaikh Ghulam Muhammad, a maternal grandson of the celebrated Shaikh Nizamm-ud-Din of Amethi and Shaikh Izzatullah were his students. Mufti Raza Ansari, *Bani-i-Dars-i-Nizami, Mulla Nizamuddin Firangi Mahali,* Aligarh, 1973, pp. 25–30.
123. Two students of Qutub-ud-Din, Shaikh Ghulam Muhammad and Izzatullah were killed by the khanzada zamindars. Muhammad Said, son of Qutub-ud-Din, *qazi* of pargana Sihali and a number of students were seriously injured. Nine hundred books including the Koran and Hadis preserved at the library of the *madrasa* were fired. The cause of khanzada zamindar attacks on the family was its close relation with Emperor Aurangzeb. M.R. Ansari, *Bani-i-Dars-i-Nizami,* pp. 25–30.
124. Mulla Qutub-ud-Din had four sons, Mulla Asad, Mulla Muhammad Said, Mulla Nizam-ud-Din and Muhammad Raza. Mulla Asad was taken in imperial services during the lifetime of his father, Mullah Nizam-ud-Din and Muhammad Raza were minors at the time of his father's death. Mullah Said went to the Mughal court to inform the emperor about his misfortune. Consequently, Aurangzeb bestowed him Firangi Mahal. M.R. Ansari, 'A Very Early Farman', PIHC, 1975, p. 355.
125. M.R. Ansari, *Bani-i-Dars-i-Nizami,* pp. 172–80.
126. NAI, 1269, 1365. In 1706 Muhammad Zaman was granted 6½ *tankas* for the establishment of a mosque consisting of *imam, khatib* and *muazzin,* ibid., 2628.
127. Allahabad Doc. Nos. 3, 7 and 8.
128. Mir Sayyid Ahmed was confirmed 534 *bighas* and 8 *biswas madad-i-maash* lands in pargana and sarkar Baharaich in 1658. Allahabad Doc. No. 791. Shaikh Izzatullah was granted 500 *bighas madad-i-maash* lands in pargana Sandila, sarkar Lucknow in 1667, ibid., No. 1190. During Aurangzeb's reign Sayyid Jamal-ud-Din was confirmed 267 *bighas* and 19 *biswas madad-i-maash* lands in pargana and sarkar Bahraich, ibid., Nos. 763, 767, 834, 844 and 878. These families were not expected to render any service to the state. Thus the grants assigned to them were charters of their social value.
129. M.A. Ansari, *Administrative Document,* Doc. No. 28. In 1710 Bibi Saleha was assigned whole village Pipla as *madad-i-maash* in pargana Gopamau, sarkar Khairabad, ibid., Doc. No. 29. Bibi Mehr Bano was assigned 350 *bighas madad-i-maash* lands in 1732 in pargana Gopamau, ibid., Doc. No. 30.
130. In 1674, 1676, 1678, 1681 and 1692, Masts. Saha Bibi, Safia, Taj Bibi, Rabia, Fatima were assigned 235, 100, 210, 200 and 210 *bighas madad-i-maash* lands respectively in pargana and sarkar Gorakhpur, NAI, 2157, 2171, 1744, 2153, 2155.

131. Allahabad Doc. No. 764.
132. In 1670 Muhammad Arif was granted 194 *bighas madad-i-maash* lands in pargana Haveli Bahraich. Allahabad Doc. No. 768. In 1676 and 1677 he was assigned *madad-i-maash* lands in the village Seha, Karampura, Hasanpur, Kantura and Kuntia in pargana Hisampur, Fakhrpur and Sailak. Allahabad Doc. Nos. 768 and 1202.
133. Ibid., Nos., 856, 1212, 1216, 1219, and 1224.
134. Ibid., Nos. 1230 and 1231.
135. Ibid., No. 846.

CHAPTER 5

The Role of the *Madad-i-Maash* Holders in Society

In the families of the *madad-i-maash* holders of the suba belonged to different social sections.[1] *Qazis*, *sajjada nashins*, and those who managed educational and religious institutions were the main beneficiaries. They were expected to render some services to the state, and to help the people. The role of *madad-i-maash* holders in society, therefore, should be seen in the background of their duties and functions.

Many families of grantees in the suba were connected with the judicial department. Besides that they also played an important role in the socio-religious and even economic life of the area. The *qazis* were instrumental in performing most of the social customs and practices of the Muslim community. They led the Friday and other congregational prayers; preached honesty and fear of God. They approved the legitimacies of marriages and registered them. They also performed important rituals in marriage and other ceremonies of the Muslims. But their duties regarding the judicial administration were for both the Muslim and the non-Muslims.[2] Besides *qazis*, other officials of the religio-judicial departments, such as *sadrs*, *muftis*, *muhatasib* and *mutawallis*, had an importants say in the socio-religious practices. Recognized as authorities in religious affairs, their services and decisions were accepted.

The grantees who managed the mosques and temples made arrangement for worship so that people could perform their religious obligations easily. The expenses of such arrangements were borne from The *madad-i-maash* assigned to them.[4] The *madad-i-maash* holders of the temples did not charge piligrimage tax and thus encouraged pilgrims to visit the temples in large number.[5] It may be mentioned that in medieval Indian society, religion occupied most significant place in the life of the people. The arrangements and facilities extended by the *madad-i-maash* holders for religious functions was indeed significant. Such arrangements included construction of mosques and employing there some functionaries. This also helped the state retain a popular image in the society. The Muslim grantees mostly belonged to the *ulema* class, an influential group in society. The activities of such persons ensured the common Muslims that religiously they were protected.

The Sufi shrines and *khanqahs* provided housing and food to the travellers, there were many *khanqahs* in Awadh where the *sajjada nashins* made such arrangements.[6] Besides, other *madad-i-maash* holders also helped travellers. In 1664 Qazi Habibullah was assigned *madad-i-maash* lands in pargana Sandila, sarkar Lucknow to help the travellers (*musafirin*).[7] Qazi Imad-ud-Din and Zakaria extended facilities to the travellers in pargana Sandila, sarkar Lucknow. Such help provided by *madad-i-maash* holders gave the travellers a bond of security. Consequently the people were encouraged to extend their social contacts. Since the *khanqahs* gave shelter to Hindus and Muslims, people got opportunity to exchange ideas. Moreover, the accommodation and food facilities enabled even the poor to travel in different areas.

Besides travellers, the grantees also gave financial support to the poor. Almost every *khanqah* provided food to them. The grantees were assigned *madad-i-maash* lands for such purposes. Such help to the poor was a common practice in the suba Awadh.[9] In this way the persons who were not in a position to meet the necessary demands of their life, being were given an opportunity to save themselves from the starvation. The grantees enabled them not to feel deprived.

The *madad-i-maash* holders played a vital role in spreading education. In medieval India the state had not founded any separate department. Generally people were given education by the *ulema*. The educational centres were mainly mosques, *khanqahs* and temples. Though the state provided financial support for the maintenance of *maktabas* and *madrasas*, the buildings for educational activity was normally the temple, mosque or *khanqah*.[10] All arrangements regarding education were made by the *madad-i-maash* holders.

The grantees made effort for the promotion of education in various ways. The *khanqahs* usually had rooms for the lodging of students. Students resided in them free of cost. The *madad-i-maash* documents bear the term *bawastey kharach-i-tualeba* 'for the expenses of the students'.[11] This attracted students of the area. It certainly helped spread education. Moreover, *khanqahs* and mosques were also built by the *madad-i-maash* holders. Though the grantees met the expenses of these buildings from the revenue yielded by the assigned *madad-i-maash* lands, the constructions of such building were supervised by the grantees themselves.[12]

The *madad-i-maash* holder of Awadh contributed to popularizing education among the masses, which led to the establishment of many educational centres of importance. Hardly was there a place in the suba where education was not imparted by the grantees. Towns like Amethi, Hargaon, Neutani, Gopamau, Khairabad, Bilgram, Sandila, Lucknow and Kakori were famous for education.[13] The family of Mulla Nizam-ud-Din, *madad-i-maash* holder of Lucknow, was famous in the field of education all over the country. Its contribution to education in the suba needs to be expanded.

During Aurangzeb's reign the family of Mulla Nizam-ud-Din shifted from pargana Sihali to Lucknow, due to the hostility of the zamindars of the pargana. Mulla Nizam-ud-Din was granted the Firangi Mahal by Aurangzeb. He converted this mahal into an advanced centre of learning.[14] The popularity of this institution increased to the extent that its curriculum, the *Silsila-i-Nizamia*,[15] was accepted as a course of instruction in large parts of Asia.[16] and it attracted students from different parts of the country. At no other place in India were such competent scholars produced. It is evident from the fact that many of the manuals used for religious instruction in the Muslim community are the products of the scholars of this *madrasa*.[17]

Primarily religious studies were carried out at the *madrasas*. The *madad-i-maash* holders, members of the priest class, were more expert in religion than any other field and therefore found it easier to impart knowledge. As studies in the religious field had great scope in medieval India, the *madad-i-maash* holders gained considerable popularity.

Secular subjects were also taught at *maktabs* and *madrasas*. The *madrasa* of Firangi Mahal was famous in the field of Islamic studies, grammar, logic, philosophy, sciences, mathematics, geometry and astronomy.[18] It is important to note that the studies in both religious and secular studies widened the scope of *madrasas*. Hindus also came there to learn in secular subjects. Thus the education facilities provided by the *madad-i-maash* holders were not limited to a particular community. This is evident from the fact that many Hindus worked in revenue and other government departments of the suba[19] and must have known Persian: in medieval India the official language was Persian and every government official had to have a knowledge of this language.

Thus, the educational activities of the *madad-i-maash* holders helped to produce experts in religious studies who served society by guiding people about the religion. *Qazis* and *muftis* who were expected to be well versed in Islamic law were largely the products of these *madrasas*. More significantly, by imparting education in non-religious studies, the grantees produced experts for the various administrative departments. It may be mentioned that the scholars produced by the *madrasas* of Awadh not only benefited the people of their own suba but also migrated to other parts of the country and imparted knowledge to the people. Many scholars of pargana Bilgram, sarkar Lucknow imparted education in Deccan.[20] In the eighteeen century Awadh became a prominent centre of learning a large number of scholars from different parts of the country and foreign countries came to Awadh to enhance their knowledge. Many Irani scholars settled in the suba also for education.

In this way educational activities of the grantees of the suba had very wide scope.[21]

It is generally believed that *madad-i-maash* holders mainly contributed in spreading conservatism in society,[22] which is subject to question. This hypothesis is perhaps based on the ground that the *madad-i-maash* holders belonged to the priest class and were involved in religious activities. It is a fact that the grantees were assigned *madad-i-maash* lands owing to be members of the religious class who were capable of maintaining society on a traditional basis. However, it does not mean that the activities of the grantees prevented progress. Some activities helped spread progressive ideas. Though the number of such grantees, who spread progressive ideas, was relatively few, the impact of their activities was great in terms of the development of their areas.

In a significant number the grantees were women in Awadh.[23] Since these women had only the *madad-i-maash* grants as sources of their livelihood, they had to control agricultural production. Moreover, for the purpose such as the renewal of the grant and to collect the sources of cultivation they had to work themselves. According to the rules *madad-i-maash* holders had to appear before the state authorities in person and had to produce reliable witnesses regarding their claim.[24] Since most of the female grantees had small holdings and normally waste cultivable lands, it was essential for them to keep an eye on the agricultural labourers for the increase of agricultural surplus. To fulfil all these requirements the women grantees had to make contact with the state and experts in agriculture. The formalities required for renewal must have relaxed, to some extent, the prevalent purdah system.[25] Moreover, females grantees also filed petitions in the royal courts when necessary.[26] This indicates that the women aware of their rights.

Women received *madad-i-maash* grants in various ways. Some women inherited the grants of their predecessors, some were assigned original grant by the state. In Awadh many women inherited the *madad-i-maash* grants of their fathers.[27] The confirmation of the grants of fathers in favour of daughters not only made the women economically self-dependant, but helped in relax the rigid Indian law of inheritance that only the males could inherit property.

Besides the property of their fathers, a large number of female grantees inherited the *madad-i-maash* grants of their husbands.[28] Women grantees who thus inherited grants of possessed sizeable lands. This enabled them to employ tenants for cultivation. By such practices they not only provided employment to the people but they also became members of agrarian society. They collected their share from the tenants, therefore, encouraged them for huge production which led to large surplus. Thus the female grantees helped to establish that women were not only meant for house keeping but they could also be instrumental in socio-economic change.

Madad-i-maash holders encouraged marketing activities in their areas. At the shrines of the Sufis the *urs*[29] was customarily celebrated. On this occasion people in large number gathered at the shrine to get the blessing of the Sufis.[30] The visitors had to perform some rituals at the time of *urs* and other religious occasions. For this purpose they needed material for presentation to the shrine.[31] Consequently some people got the opportunity to set-up shops neat the shrines to sell the goods required for the purposes of worship. Moreover, the religious functions also led to the establishment of shops for the essential commodities for daily use of the people. It may be mentioned that people generally visited the shrines once a week, especially on Thursday. More importantly, during the medieval period the organization of periodic markets near Sufi shrines was a general practice. In a situation where a large number of people had limited resources, such religious functions, organized by the *madad-i-maash* holders at different occasions at the shrines, stimulated a retail trade. Since in Awadh, a large number of shrines existed,[32] religious ceremonies played a vital role in the development of local-level marketing. Moreover, the establishment of a market near a shrines meant a sources of income for artisans.[33] It provided work for petty craftsmen who made wooden goods or prayer caps, etc.[34]

The *madad-i-maash* holders planted orchards on a large scale.[35] They were given grants specifically for this purpose.[36] In Awadh the grant holders planted and supervised the growth of mango, guava and other fruits.[37] These groves helped strengthen the rural economy,[38] and also provided some relief to the people during the summer season. In medieval India transportation system was not so developed that people could use it in their daily life. Usually they travelled on foot. Such groves became places of rest for travellers in both summer and rainy seasons. Moreover, it was a general practice among the Muslims to build the graves among groves of fruit trees.[39] Generally the control of graveyards was in the hands of *madad-i-maash* holders and the income from the fruits was appropriated by them.[40] It may be mentioned that the fruits from orchards were not only consumed by their owners, but these were also sold for profit.[41] Since orchards were a source of income, it seems that the grantees might have been encouraged to grow trees in large number. Thus with the plantation of orchards, *madad-i-maash* holders improved their own economic condition and also provided fruit to the locality.

The *madad-i-maash* holders constructed wells and inns. Though they were assigned *madad-i-maash* lands by the state for these purposes, other formalities for the completion of these constructions were completed by the grantees. The materials for such works were arranged by them. Such activities of the grantees helped the people in two ways, first, the wells provided sufficient water for the people of neighbouring areas, the inns acted as rest house for the travellers and other needy persons. Second, the wells also helped in the development of cultivation. It is important to note that wells were one of the important sources of irrigation. It seems that the construction of such wells might have encouraged the plantation of gardens. Since the wells were often dug by the grantees in inhabited areas it might also have helped in the growing of vegetables.

The grantees in their own economic interest converted unworked lands into cultivation. This process also helped in the extension of the cultivated area. The yield from the assigned holdings was an addition to general production of the area. In the absence of such practice, they would have appropriated the surplus from already cultivated lands. The large size of holdings of the grantees generated higher surplus, effecting favourably the economic life of the region. This process on the whole helped in the economic development of the concerned region.

The *madad-i-maash* holders played an important role in spreading urban culture in the areas where they settled. In Awadh a majority of *madad-i-maash* holders were Muslims of the Shaikh and Sayyids families and were generally from urban areas. But when they were assigned *madad-i-maash* grants in village their interest shifted to rural areas. It has been already mentioned that the *madad-i-maash* holders imparted education, organized religious ceremonies and encouraged marketing activities. Such activities were helpful in the expansion of urban culture in the suba. Moreover, the Muslim grantees settled in rural area had direct contact with the *qazis, sadrs,* and other officials of the religio-judicial departments. It may be mentioned that these officials held office, generally, in urban areas, therefore, their connection with the *madad-i-maash* holders of rural areas helped in spreading culture in the villages. The *dargahs* of the Sufis were usually visited by the nobles. The nobles were from urban areas and therefore, their visit of the *dargahs* in rural areas would have encouraged urban culture.[42]

The most important role of the grantees was that they helped establish social harmony. It has been mentioned that non-Muslim also got education in the *madrasas* established by the Muslim grantees. Though the main purpose of non-Muslim students of the *madrasas* was to learn the Persian language so that could gets jobs in public offices, at the same time both Muslims and non-Muslim got the opportunity to exchange ideas; they came to know the cultures of each other and to establish social contact.

Moreover, the *madad-i-maash* holders who were descendants of Sufis made significant contributions to bring the people of both Hindu and Muslim communities close to each other. In Awadh generally, the Sufi saints belonged to Chisti *silsila* who believed in universal brotherhood and were more concerned with the common masses.[43] They served the people irrespective of religion and caste. They developed the idea of toleration and established harmony in society. It is evident from an instruction of Muinuddin Chisti, the founder of Chisti *silsila* in India that was recorded by Amir Khurd, the author of *Siyar-ul-Aula*, 'River like generosity, sun like affection and earth like hospitality are three qualities which endear a man to God'.[44] Such preaching was certainly helpful in creating healthy atmosphere in the suba.

The Sufi and their descendants started their life according to the customs and traditions of those areas where they settled. It is important to note that the reason of the success of *khanqahs* of medieval India was that the *sajjada nashin* adjusted to society without attacking the social values of those areas.[45] It is known that some Sufis adopted the life of farmers.[46]

Besides Sufi saints and *sajjada nashin*, other categories of *madad-i-maash* holders of the suba also adjusted to the customs and traditions of the areas. *Madad-i-maash* holders who prior to the assignment of grant land had been urban based and were not expert in agriculture, had to take help from the people of the villages. Such contacts led to the cultural synthesis. The *madad-i-maash* holders spread urban culture in rural areas, while they adopted certain festivals and customs of the villages.[47]

Moreover, with the settlement of Muslim *madad-i-maash* holders in rural areas Hindus came to have contact with them. Consequently people of both communities became aware of the religion of each other.

The above-mentioned activities of *madad-i-maash* holders indicate that they played a constructive role in the socio-economic development of the suba. However, this had another side also. There were some *madad-i-maash* holders in the suba who created problems and became a source of social problems.

Some grantees, who belonged to the influential section of society and had sizeable lands under their control, were involved in illegal practices. Among such grantees *qazis* were greatest problem creators. They tried to establish their supremacy in their areas, and also were involved in illegal occupation of land. In 1679, Ahmed, a grantee of village Kantura, pargana Fakhrpur, sarkar Bahraich complained that Qazi Wali Muhammad and his father had illegally occupied his *madad-i-maash* lands.[48] The subedar, therefore ordered some government officials with some army men to proceed to village Kantura and demarcate the boundaries of the disputed lands. Despite government instruction to him, Qazi Wali Muhammad did not stop his unlawful activities. On the contrary he, with his father and some other persons of the area, mobilized a resistance.[49] Qazi Wali Muhammad and his relations indulged in several other illegal activities.[50] Such evidence is important as it shows the defiant attitude of the *qazis* against the state, and shows the tendency of illegal occupation of lands by them. More importantly, the illegal occupation of *madad-i-maash* lands by grantees indicates that the *qazis* had little public sympathy. It may be mentioned that generally both the *qazi* and other *madad-i-maash* holders belonged to the *ulema* group. Their activities indicate that some of them usurped lands of other and tried to become strong in the area.

Some *qazis* often created problems for the zamindars. During Aurangzeb's reign the zamindars of a village of sarkar Bahraich complained that a certain *qazi* forcibly realized their *rusum-i-zamindari*[51] and also seized their lands.[52] It seems that even the zamindars who were strong as a class at the local level had to face a challenge from the *qazis*. Besides, the *qazis* also created problems for the peasants.[53] Such activities were obstructions in both the social and economic development of the area. The *qazis* who were expected to mould society towards progress became exploiters in the eyes of the people. Since they were judicial officers, people had to appear in their offices for the settlement of disputed cases. But due to illegal practices of the *qazis*, it became difficult for people to trust them and is also increased problems of the people. Moreover, the attempts of the *qazis* to share surplus of zamindars, and cultivators were dangerous for agricultural production. It may be pointed out that zamindars and cultivators had a major role in agricultural production and were revenue paying classes. When they were obstructed by those who were neither producers, nor revenue payers, agricultural productions would have been discouraged.

The *qazis* interfered not only with the rights of the *madad-i-maash* holders and zamindars and cultivators but they had also become corrupt.[54] They did not perform their duties properly. It deserves to be mentioned that at the time of the appointment of a *qazi* the state gave instruction to him to perform his duties honestly. However, the *qazis*, being member of the *ulema*, had large numbers of supporters in their areas,[55] and could produce false witnesses when the occasion demanded. Many rituals in marriages and festivals were performed by *qazis* and it was difficult for the people of the area to make petitions against them at the royal court. Those who had the resources could bribe the *qazis*.[56] Moreover, the illegal practices of *qazis* were also problem for the administration.

Besides the *qazis* some other *madad-i-maash* holders also created disturbances in society. They unlawfully occupied the lands of others, and prevented their co-shares occupying lands assigned.[57] In the eighteenth century generally the *madad-i-maash* holders started to strengthen their power in their areas by acquiring *zamindari* rights. Consequently they came into conflict with the zamindars.[58]

Thus, on the basis of the above study it seems that the bulk of the grantees of the suba played a positive and helpful role, for which they were assigned the grant. However, though few in number, some grantees were defiant and remained a source of continued political problems.

NOTES

1. The *qazis* performed judicial duties such as determining the boundaries of agricultural and other areas, issuing penal code orders (*Izara-i-Tazirat*), protecting public properties and solving disputes. Allahabad Doc. No. 254. For their duties in detail, see Zamiruddin, 'Institutions of *qazis* under the Mughal', R. Bilgrami, *Medieval India: A Miscellany*, vol. I.
2. Allahabad Doc. No. 254.
3. The *qazis* attested document dealing with the transfer of lands, verified and attested accounts before they were forwarded to higher authorities or kept as local records. N.A. Siddiqui, *Land Revenue Administration Under the Mughal (1700–1750)*, Bombay, 1970, p. 14. Thus the duties of the *qazis* were not confined to religious affairs, but extended to agrarian administration and public properties.
4. A *madad-i-maash* document indicates that in 1706 the income from *madad-i-maash* lands were utilized for the maintenance of mosque with an *imam, khatib* and *muzzin* in pargana Sandila, sarkar Lucknow, Allahabad Doc. No. 2608.
5. M.A. Ansari (ed)., *Administrative Documents of Mughal India*, Delhi, 1983. No. 35.
6. See the list of shrines mentioned in Chapter 4, 'Concentration and Dispersal'.
7. NAI, 1270.
8. Ibid. 1273, 2161 and 1652.
9. In 1675 Qazi Imad-ud-Din was given 294 *bighas madad-i-maash* lands in pargana Nimkhar, sarkar Khairabad for the maintenance of the poor. NAI, 1272. In 1717, Shaikh Karamullah was assigned 235 *bighas* lands to help the poor in pargana Sandila, sarkar Lucknow. Ibid. 1050. In 1683 Izzatullah was given *madad-i-maash* lands in pargana Firozabad, sarkar Bahraich for the maintenance of the *khanqah*. Allahabad Doc. No. 804. In *madad-i-maash* documents for the maintenance of the poor the term has been used *ba wastey kharach-i-faqir*. Rafat Bilgrami, 'Some Mughal Revenue Grants', *Medieval India, A Miscellany*, vol. II, p. 323. NAI, 1272, 2160. In medieval Europe the poor were helped by the monasteries. C.A. Bayly, *Rulers, Townsmen and Bazaars, North Indian Society in the Age of British Expansion (1770–1870)*. Cambridge, 1983, p. 129. Thus it can be assumed that it was customary for the religious institutions of the medieval world to provide financial support to the poor.

10. S.M. Jaffar, *Education in Muslim India*, Delhi, 1972, pp. 16–19, 28.
11. NAI, 1050, 1272, 1582, 1652. Rafat Bilgrami, 'Some Mughal Revenue Grants', *Medieval India: A Miscellany*, vol. II, pp. 319, 323. The houses of *ulema* were important centres of education providing free boarding and lodging to students. N.N. Law, *Promotion of Learning in India during Mohammedan Rule*, London, 1916, p. 164.
12. Qazi Imad-ud-Din and Muhammad Zaman were given *madad-i-maash* lands by Aurangzeb for the construction of *khanqahs* and mosques in pargana Sandila, sarkar Lucknow. NAI 1651, 2608. Qazi Daim was granted 5 *bighas madad-i-maash* land for the establishment of *khanqahs* and mosques. Iqbal Husain, 'Calendar of Khairabad Documents', *Islamic Culture*, vol. 53, no. 1, p. 47.
13. Maulana Hakim Sayyid Abdul Hai, *Islami Ulum-o-Funun Hindustan Mein*, Azamgarh, 1969, pp. 12, 16; S.M. Jaffar, *Education in Muslim India*, pp. 17–18.
14. Firangi Mahal was built by Dutch merchant in Lucknow. N.N. Law, *Promotion of Learning in India during Muhammadan Rule*, London, 1916, p. 188.
15. *Silsila-i-Nizamia* was an Arabic *silsila*, a chain or series which enlarged the scope of education by incorporating social and physical sciences into the curriculum. Abdul Halim Sharar, *Lucknow: The Last Phase of an Oriental Culture*, London, 1975, pp. 38–9.
16. Ibid., p. 39.
17. Ibid., p. 94.
18. Abdul Halim Sharar, *Lucknow: The Last Phase*, p. 94.
19. K.P. Srivastava (ed.), *Mughal Farman (1504–1706)*, Lucknow, 1974, pp. 31, 57, 58, 62. Allahabad Doc. Nos. 873, 874, 877, 1179, 1184. Generally the posts of the qanungos were held by the Hindus in the suba. Ibid. Nos. 878, 1234, 1255.
20. S.A.A. Rizvi, *Shah Waliullah and His Times*, Canberra, 1980, p. 185.
21. Ibid., p. 388. The contributions of the *madrasa* of Firangi Mahal can be estimated from the fact that in the first decade of century the number of students increased rapidly. This led to the increase in the *madad-i-maash* lands to the *madrasa* in addition to earlier grant. The Emperor Bahadur Shah (1707–12) was impressed with the progress of *madrasa* and extended additional aid of rupees two per day to it. M.R. Ansari, *Bani-i-Dars-i-Nizami*, pp. 170–8.
22. Richard M. Eaton, *Sufis of Bijapur, 1300–1700*, New Jersey, 1978, p. 217.
23. A list of women grantees has been given which indicates the nature of their land holdings. Appendix C.
24. Allahabad Doc. Nos. 9, 761, 778, 796, 813, 843 and 859.
25. An order of Aurangzeb indicates that he exempted female grantees from attending the *jashn* and other ceremonies. S.M. Azizuddin Husain, '*Kalimat-i-Aurangzeb*: A source of Aurangzeb's Reign', PIHC, 1979, p. 317.
26. In 1666, Sayyid Usman forcibly occupied the grant of Bibi Lazyat in pargana Hisampur, sarkar Bahraich. Bibi Lazyat petitioned against the illegal occupation by Usman. He was ordered by the state to surrender the occupied grant to Bibi Lazyat. Allahabad Doc. No. 1189.

27. In 1661 Mst. Chappa was confirmed 45 *bighas* grant lands of her father Abdul Qadir in pargana Sadrpur, sarkar Khairabad. Allahabad Doc. No. 796. In 1685 Mst. Rafi was assigned 20 *bighas madad-i-maash* lands of her father Shaikh Qutub-ud-Din in pargana Sadrpur, sarkar Khairabad. Ibid., 814. In 1694 Mst. Bekhi was confirmed sizeable *madad-i-maash* grants of her father Abdur Razzaq in pargana Mallawan, sarkar Lucknow. Ibid., 94.
28. Ibid., 813.
29. *Urs*: the festival commemorating the death date of a Sufi, normally the most important festival at a *dargah*.
30. Richard M. Eaton, *Sufis of Bijapur*, p. xxiv.
31. Ibid.
32. *District Gazetteers of United Provinces* indicate that every pargana of Awadh had Sufi shrines.
33. C.A. Bayly, *Rulers, Towns and Bazaars*, p. 43.
34. Ibid.
35. Irfan Habib, 'Potentialities of Capitalistic Development in the Economy of Mughal India', *An Enquiry*, Delhi, 1971, p. 18.
36. NAI, 1393.
37. C.A. Baylay, *Rulers, Towns and Bazaars*, p. 43.
38. Ibid.
39. Irfan Habib, *Agrarian System of Mughal India*, Bombay, 1963, p. 49.
40. In 1684, 17 *bighas madad-i-maash* lands were assigned to Qazi Imad-ud-Din in pargana Sandila, sarkar Lucknow for the construction of well. NAI, 1651. In 1719 Zain-ul-Abidin was granted 4 *bighas* in pargana and sarkar Gorakhpur for the construction of well. Ibid., 2173 and 2447.
41. Iqbal Husain, 'Calendar of Khairabad Documents', *Islamic Culture*, vol. 53, no. 1, p. 48.
42. According to N.A. Siddiqui, 'The Muslim (grantees) who settled down in the village had direct contact with the urban culture of the provincial or district headquarters were thus in position to carry the Muslim urban culture in remote interior areas of the country', *Land Revenue Administration*, p. 133.
43. A. Rashid, *Society and Culture in Medieval India*, Calcutta, 1969, p. 178.
44. Compare A. Rashid, *Society and Culture*, p. 179. *Siyar-ul-Aulia* contains biographical notes on the saints of the Chisti order in India. It was written during the reign of Firoz Shah by Sayyid Mubarak Kirmani alias Amir Khurd.
45. According to K.A. Nizami, 'The success of these khanqahs depended very largely on Shaikh's ability to adjust and adopt himself to the mental climate of a particular region. Unless they identified themselves with the problems of the people, their worries, their hopes and their aspirations these khanqahs could not gain the confidence of the people', *Studies in Medieval Indian Society*, Allahabad, 1966, p. 82.
46. Ibid., p. 83.
47. According to N.A. Siddiqui, 'They (grantees) were considerably influenced by local customs and some of these got absorbed into their own culture. With the

passage of time they began to participate in local festivals not because they identified themselves with their ideological foundations but only as customary social behaviour which gave them opportunity of enjoying themselves by sharing festivities with persons who although, they professed different religion their long life companions in facing the common problems of rural life. Similarly the simple minded Hindus in the villages came to know and understand Muslim culture and religion as practised and observed by Muslim in their daily life'. N.A. Siddiqui, *Land Revenue Administration,* p. 133.

48. *Mofid-ul-Insha,* a collection of letters drafted in the closing years of Aurangzeb's reign shows that the relations between faujdar and *qazis* were not cordial. It records the charges against the *qazis* levelled by the faujdar of Cooch Behar, 'The qazis on the whole were a lot of wicked people who specialized in villification and mischief mongering. They had made up their mind to maintain an attitude of hostility towards the administration and were bent upon implicating the faujdar in charge of a very grave nature'. Compare, N.A. Siddiqui, 'Pulls and Pressures on the Faujdar Under the Mughals', PIHC, 1967, Pt. I, p. 247. 49. Allahabad Doc. No. 1202.

50. In 1672, a *madad-i-maash* holder of village Kapurpur, pargana Hisampur, sarkar Bahraich, complained that Qazi Wali Muhammad occupied 120 *bighas* of his *madad-i-maash* lands. Ibid., No. 782. A document shows that Qazi Wali Muhammad also occupied 5,375 *bighas* in pargana Hisampur in spite of the fact that he was granted 750 *bighas* lands only. Ibid., No. 782. In 1676 two *madad-i-maash* holders Sayyid Muhammad Arif and Sayyid Ghayasuddin complained that Qazi Wali Muhammad and his father had illegally occupied 1,000 *bighas* of their *madad-i-maash* lands in village Kantura, pargana Fakhrpur, sarkar Bahraich. Ibid., No. 851/1, 2.

51. *Rusum-i-zamindari* was the customary exactions of the zamindars.

52. Irfan Habib, *Agrarian System,* pp. 144–5.

53. During Aurangzeb's reign Qazi Wali Muhammad forcibly collected Rs. 300 from the cultivators in pargana Hisampur, sarkar Bahraich, Allahabad Doc. No. 782.

54. According to Abul Fazal, '. . . the *Qazis* were in a habit of taking bribes from grant holders. The qazis who wear a turban of respectability, but are bad at heart, who wear long sleeves, but fall short in sense.' *Ain-i-Akbari,* vol. I (English trans.), p. 279. A document of Aurangzeb's reign indicate that a *qazi* of pargana Batala, suba Lahore, harassed the people so badly that they had to leave the town. J.S. Grewal, *Miscellaneous Articles,* Amritsar, 1974, pp. 46, 49.

55. The diwan gave certain instructions to the newly appointed *qazis* 'Be just, be honest, be impartial. Hold trials in the presence of the parties and at the court house and seat of government (muhukama). Do not accept presents from the people of the place. Where you serve, nor attend entertainment given by anybody.' Sir J.N. Sarkar, *Mughal Administration,* Calcutta, 1963, p. 23. However, these instructions hardly were rarely followed. In 1671 Aurangzeb learnt that the *qazis* of the province of Gujarat took holidays for three days in a week and on

others attended the governors' court. The emperor ordered a stop to such practices and decreed that they may only have Friday as a holiday and should attend governors' courts on Wednesdays. Ibid., pp. 99–100.

56. According to Bernier, a French traveller, '. . . if justice be ever administered, it is among the lower classes, among persons who being equally poor have no means of corrupting the judges (*qazis*) and buying false witnesses'. He further observes, 'if the party really in the wrong had possessed means of putting a couple of crowns in the lands of *kadi* or his clerks and of buying with the same two false witnesses he would have indisputably have gained his cause or prolonged as long as he pleased'. *Travels in the Mogul Empire, 1665–68*, trans. by Archibald Constable, Delhi, 1968, pp. 237–8.
57. Allahabad Doc. Nos. 1201 and 1189.
58. Allahabad Doc. Nos. 1315 and 1565.

CHAPTER 6

The Position of *Madad-i-Maash* Holders of the Suba

Since second half of seventeenth century the *madad-i-maash* grantees of Awadh remained important in socio-economic and political life of the suba. Though they depended on the state for their livelihood, the attitude of the state towards them indicates that their assignments were not merely an act of charity on the part of state rather the state was itself interested in the creation of such a class. It prayed for the welfare of the state and the emperor.[1] Thus the state had its own interest in extending its favour to this class. The state tried to win the support of the people with the help of these grantees who had close connection with different sections of the society. The state's favour enabled them to strengthen their position in their respective area.

Madad-i-maash holders were considered as experts in the branch of religious studies, therefore, the state had the great advantage in patronizing these people. The state took the help of grantees in legitimizing its rights of the imposition and collection of taxes from the people.

The legitimization of the policies of state by the *madad-i-maash* holders was enough to implement them in the empire. The grantees such as *sajjada nashin, qazis* and others related to religious-judicial department had large following, therefore, they were the strong elements in the society to protect the interest of the state. In lieu of their services, the state was expected to make the grantees to fulfil their needs.

Besides taking the help of the grantees for the support of policies, the religious merit of the grantees also tempted the royal authorities to get their blessings. It may be mentioned that royal authorities also belonged to orthodox families. They were more religious than the rest of the people of the society. They also visited the *dargahs* to get the blessings of Sufis for the betterment of their empire as well as the members of their own family. It is evident that even Akbar in 1561 visited the *dargah* of Khawaja Muinuddin Chisti[2] and Salim Chisti to get their blessings to have a son.

Like Akbar other Mughal emperors also respected the Sufis and their *dargahs.* Even Aurangzeb was a disciple of a Sufi Khawaja Muhammad Masum.[3] It is important to note that besides *sajjada nashin, madad-i-maash* holders of other categories were also connected with the *dargahs* of the Sufis. The recognition of the importance of Sufis and their *dargahs* by the Mughal emperors helped the *madad-i-maash* holders to win the support of the other authorities of local areas in strengthening their position. It may be mentioned that in Awadh a number of the *dargahs* existed during Mughal period,[4] as such the grantees of the suba had considerable advantage in getting the support of the state.[5]

There are reference that the Mughal emperor believed that the harassment of *madad-i-maash* holders was unfortunately for their empire and royal families. For instance Shahjahan in 1634 ordered the cancellation of the grants of those assignees who were involved in forgery. After sometimes of the issuing of this order his daughter Jahanara was seriously injured by fire, Shahjahan believed that his daughter was injured due to the resumption of such grants.[6] Such beliefs of the emperors contributed to bring great concessions to the *madad-i-maash* holders. Thus it can be assumed that the state's recognition to the religious merit of the grantees and its efforts to get their social support enabled the grantees to make themselves politically strong. In Awadh many grantees were not only famous for their religious merit at local level but they were quite popular in other parts of the country for their knowledge in religious studies.[7] Such grantees, therefore, were helped them in establishing considerable influence in society.

It has been mentioned in last chapter that the travellers, scholars and destitute persons were helped by the grantees. Some other public welfare works were also done by them.[8] Though the income of such grants given by the state enabled the grantees to undertake the welfare works, the general beneficiaries, however, felt directly obliged to the grantees. It may be mentioned that in Awadh due to their benevolent activities grantees were quite capable of receiving a large sum of funds from the government for public welfare works.[9] By performing public welfare duties they created their own followers in the society. Consequently, the grantees became popular among the masses.

Generally the *madad-i-maash* holders belonged to *ulema* class. Most of the religious duties and ceremonies were performed by them. In many customary practices the grantees played the leading role.[10] More importantly these people were interpreter of Islamic laws.[11] During medieval period religious ties were so strong that hardly any person could challenge the established customary religious practices. It is interesting to note that both lower and upper classes, the grantees became successful in making their connection with the majority of people of society. Having a large gatherings around them the grantees also became more powerful than other elite group of society. Even in some cases an economically weak grantee was more influential in his community than an economically well off zamindar of the area. For instance, in marriage ceremonies of Muslims the completion of *nikah* was the single monoply of the *qazis.*[12] Without performing this custom marriage was incomplete. Therefore, the zamindars also depended on the *qazis* for the completion of such ceremonies. Zamindars' denial of the religious merit of the *qazis* and other persons of *ulema* class could led to the social opposition of them. Consequently the grantees being religious leader acquired prestigious position in society.[13]

In Awadh majority of *madad-i-maash* holders belonged to Muslim community. However, it does not mean that their connection were limited to the people of their own community. It has been mentioned earlier that a large number of *madad-i-maash* holders of the suba were *sajjada nashins.* One of the important functions of these *sajjada nashins* was to organize *urs.* It is important to mention that at occasions of the *urs* people of both Muslim and Hindu communities gathered at the shrine to get the blessings of the saint. The *sajjada nashins* being the head of these places had the moral support of these large number of people of different sections and different communities. Since the Sufis were not critical of other religions they succeeded to create a large number of their followers among Hindus also. It deserves to mention that the Sufis preached the concept of equality, but they did not criticize the existing varna system in Hindu community. Consequently the Sufis and their shrines received a considerable respect from the Hindus.[14] Even some Brahmans, the pillars of Hinduism, were the followers of Sufi shrines.[15] It may be noted that besides *sajjada nashins,* the shrines also consisted of other petty *madad-i-maash* holders who were called *mujavirs* therefore, these *madad-i-maash* holders established an unbreakable connections with significant number of the visitors of the shrine.

In Awadh bulk of the grantees belonged to the Sayyids and Shaikhs groups of Muslim community.[16] The people of these groups were considered pious men and descendants of Prophet Muhammad. Therefore, the grantees of the suba were given importance because of belonging to noble lineage. It was difficult for the people of other groups of Muslim community to challenge the authority of Shaikhs and Sayyids. The importance of these groups in Muslim community can be judged from the fact that in any disputed case the opinions of the Shaikhs and Sayyids were more effective than other group.[17] Consequently the people preferred to associate them with these 'Pious men'. The Shaikhs and Sayyids who held these grants were more respected in society as compared to Shaikhs and Sayyids of any other professions. This was because the grantees on the one hand performed religious duties, on the other they were by birth of superior lineage, whereas other persons of the same groups had only the latter quality. Therefore, the majority in the area tried to have social affiliation with the grantees. With such a social backing the grantees also became politically important. Thus, it can be assumed that socio-religiously the grantees of the suba occupied the same place in Muslim community as the Brahmans in Hindu community.[18]

Many *madad-i-maash* holders of the suba were assigned religio-judicial office. The hdders of such offices, as *qazis*, *sadrs*, *muftis*[19] and *muhatasibs*, were grant holders.[20] During the Mughal period, particularly in the later seventeenth century, these offices had become hereditary.[21] Even an undeserving son of *qazi* was appointed his successor. In 1718 Muhammad Ahsan, who was only 15 years old, was proclaimed by the people as successor of his father Qazi Muhammad Nasir of pargana Bilgrama, sarkar Lucknow. As he was incapable of performing the duties of *qazi* independently, one Inayatullah was asked to assist him as his naib. After two years, the state recognized him as bonafide *qazi*.[22]

The practice of appointing *qazis* on a hereditary rule was not common only at places where such families were powerful but even such areas where their position was relatively weak.[23] One incident of 1676–7 indicates that Wali Muhammad, the *qazi* of pargana Hisampur, sarkar Bahraich, was dismissed due to a conflict with the zamindars and the grantees of the area, even he excercised his claim over the grant lands which he had received against his pay in lieu of his services as *qazi*.[24] More importantly, if a *qazi* had no son to succeed him as *qazi* even his *madad-i-maash* grant was renewed to his daughters or relatives. In 1674, Qazi Abdur Razzaq of pargana Sandila, sarkar Lucknow had no son and his daughter Mst. Bakhi inherited the *madad-i-maash* including a house and a garden.[25] It is important to note that while women were not eligible for the appointment as *qazi*, they received the *madad-i-maash* grants of their ancestors who were assigned these in lieu of service. This indicates that the families of the *qazis* had acquired hereditary rights over both the offices and the *madad-i-maash* grants. Such practices obviously brought rich dividends in terms of land occupation and social influence.[26]

In many parganas of Awadh, *madad-i-maash* holders alienated a significant part of total revenue (*jama*). In 9 out of 133 parganas of the suba, grantees appropriated more than 10 per cent of total revenue.[27] An analysis of the *sayurghal* statistics in the *Ain-i-Akbari* indicates that a considerable parts of the two blocks of high *sayurghal* figures of modern Uttar Pradesh were concentrated in the Mughal province of Awadh.[28] It may be pointed out that generally *madad-i-maash* lands were assigned in waste (cultivable) lands. As the grantees of Awadh occupied revenue yielding or already productive areas it indicates that they appropriated significant surplus produces.

Besides occupation of an important part of *jama* by some grantees, many *madad-i-maash* holders of Awadh also had big holdings of *madad-i-mash* lands. A number of grantees had more than 200 *bighas* of lands under their control. A list of such *madad-i-maash* holdings in the suba is given in the Table 2.

Table 2 indicates that the above-mentioned grantees had sizeable lands under their control. This made them comfortable and also helped in accumulating wealth. It is evident from that Qazi Abdur Razzaq, a grantee of pargana Sandila, sarkar Lucknow built houses, and a mosque, and purchased some garden.[29] Another case indicates that Izzatuallah, a *madad-i-maash* holder of pargana Haveli Lucknow, possessed gardens, wells and tanks.[30]

The *madad-i-maash* holders who held large *madad-i-maash* grants and possessed enough wealth and power, acquired *zamindari* rights. In 1672 Mir Sayyid Ahmed, a grantee of pargana and sarkar Bahraich purchased the *zamindari* rights of a village.[31] In 1677 Mir Sayyid Muhammad a grantee of pargana and sarkar Bahraich purchased the *zamindari* rights of a village.[32] Sayyid Mir Muhammad Arif, a prominent *madad-i-maash* holder of sarkar Bahraich purchased the *zamindari* rights of many villages.[33] In eighteenth century the successor of Qazi Daim of pargana and sarkar Khairabad acquired *zamindari* rights in village Panwaria on the basis of *madad-i-maash* lands assigned to them during Aurangzeb's reign.[34] The available references show that the acquisition of *zamindari* rights by the *madad-i-maash* holders of the suba were a late seventeenth-century development. In the eighteenth century this practice was followed in this area on large scale.[35]

However, it may be noted that the *zamindaris* of the grantees were

TABLE 1: THE GRANTEES HAVING 200 *BIGHS* OR MORE LANDS

S. No.	*Name of the grantee*	*Year*	*Size of holdings*	*Pargana*	*Sources*
1	Mir Sayyid Ahmed	1658	534 *bighas,* 8 *biswas*	Bahraich	Allahabad Doc. 791
2	Mst. Bibi Jan and others	1662	2,220 *bighas,* 8 *biswas*	Hisampur	Allahabad Doc. 169
3	Sayyid Jamal-ud-Din	1663	267 *bighas,* 19 *biswas*	Bahraich	Allahabad Doc. 764
4	Sayyid Shukurullah	1664	200 *bighas,* 19 *biswas*	Sailak	Allahabad Doc. 848
5	Shaikh Mah Mahmud	1669	240 *bighas,* 19 *biswas*	Lucknow	Allahabad Doc. 204
6	Habibullah and Pir Muhammad	1669	592 *bighas,* 19 *biswas*	Gorakhpur	NAI 2154
7	Qazi Wali Muhammad	1671	5,375 *bighas,* 19 *biswas*	Hisampur	Allahabad Doc. 781
8	Mst. Rabia	1674	200 *bighas,* 19 *biswas*	Bahraich	Allahabad Doc. 771
9	Mst. Bibi Makhan	1674	300 *bighas,* 19 *biswas*	Bahraich	Allahabad Doc. 174
10	Sayyid Ali	1674	200 *bighas,* 19 *biswas*	Hisampur	Allahabad Doc. 171
11	Mir Sayyid Uskan	1676	608 *bighas,* 19 *biswas*	Fakhrpur	Allahabad Doc. 766
12	Muhammad Mahdi Hasan	1676	645 *bighas,* 19 *biswas*	Hisampur	Allahabad Doc. 179
13	Mst. Rabia	1684	300 *bighas,* 19 *biswas*	Maghar	NAI 2160
14	Shaikh Ziauddin	1688	300 *bighas,* 19 *biswas*	Sailak	Allahabad Doc. 846
15	Mir Sayyid Muhammad Arif	1688	990 *bighas,* 19 *biswas*	Bahraich	Allahabad Doc. 1300
16	Mst. Dulari	1695	Villages Korsanda and Malabir, 19 *biswas*	Gopamau	M.A. Ansari Administrative Doc. 28
17	Sayyid Yahya	1700	200 *bighas,* 19 *biswas*	Sailak	Allahabad Doc. 860
18	Sayyid Faizullah	1702	790 *bighas,* 19 *biswas*	Hisampur	Allahabad Doc. 173
19	Bibi Saleha	1714	200 *bighas,* 19 *biswas*	Sadrpur	Allahabad Doc. 825
20	Muhammad Naim	1716	265 *bighas,* 19 *biswas*	Sandila	NAI 1652
21	Shaikh Karamullah	1717	235 *bighas,* 19 *biswas*	Sandila	NAI 1050
22	Abul Khair	1730	1,836 *bighas,* 19 *biswas*	Daryabad	Allahabad Doc. 32.
23	Hafiz Abdul Ali	1755	A Village	Sandila	NAI 1399
24	Sayyid Abbas Ali	1767	305 *bighas,* 19 *biswas*	Bahraich	Allahabad Doc. 824

treated more generously by the state than the *zamindaris* of an original zamindar.[36] The *madad-i-maash* holders seem to have been exempted from certain levies on their *zamindari* holdings. A document of 1676–7 shows that the taluqa of Mir Sayyid Ahmed, a grantee of pargana Hisampur, sarkar Bahraich, was exempt from the levy and the jagirdars of the area were instructed not to collect cess from the taluqa of the said grantee.[37] Another document of Aurangzeb's reign records that tappa Mubarakpur in sarkar Bahraich as taluqa of both *madad-i-maash* and the *milkiyat-o-zamindari* of Mir Sayyid Muhammad Arif.[38] These instances indicate that the grantees of Awadh accumulated enough wealth to purchase landed property. Though, in theory, they were a class which was expected to pray for the preservation of the everlasting empire, but in practice, particularly in eighteenth century, this class became more active in the expansion of its own property.

The purchase of *zamindari* rights by the grantees of the suba clearly indicates that the grantees were economically well off, and intended to enter the landed elite by increasing their property such efforts were not only helpful to the grantees in accumulation of wealth, but became also beneficial in creating large number of supporters in particular areas. They were respected persons in the area owing to their religious merit, but when they purchased large holdings they became able to employ many tenants. Since they had purchased *zamindari* rights, the grantees were entitled to collect customary exactions (*rusum-i-zamindari*) from the peasants of the area. Such exactions were beneficial for the grantees and seem to have inspired the grantees to increase the areas of *zamindari* on a macro scale.

Besides purchasing *zamindari* rights, some grantees of the suba also converted their *madad-i-maash* lands into *zamindari.* Such practice seems to have been intensified in the eighteenth century. Two documents of 1763–4 indicates that Shah Muhammad Akbar converted his *madad-i-maash* lands into *zamindari* and he sold his *satrahi*[39] rights to one Shaikh Ruhul Amin in pargana Sandila, sarkar Lucknow.[40] The successors of Qazi Daim acquired *zamindari* rights on their *madad-i-maash* lands in pargana and sarkar Khairabad.[41] The objective behind the conversion of *madad-i-maash* lands in *zamindari* seems to have been power at local level. This is established fact that zamindars were more powerful as a class than any other class of the area, and they had more rights than the latter. Such practice was also helpful in the expansion of their area of lands. As simple *madad-i-maash* holders they could not be authorized to collect the revenue of a particular area, but as zamindars they could collect revenue (land) and thus they exercise their rights in settlement of disputed cases of their areas. Thus theoretically they were *madad-i-maash* holders, but practically they acted as zamindars.[42]

Having accumulated wealth, the grantees of the suba aspired to increase their influence in their areas by taking lands of others on a contract basis (*ijara*). In 1678, the jagir of Namdar Khan was farmed out to Mir Sayyid Ahmed for Rs. 463/8 in pargana Hisampur, sarkar Bahraich. Sayyid Muhammad Arif, a *madad-i-maash* holder of pargana Bahraich held some villages on *ijara* for Rs. 330/10 during Aurangzeb's reign.[43] Moreover, these grantees also purchased sizeable lands in the latter half of seventeenth century.[44] In 1672 Mir Sayyid Ahmed purchased lands for residential purposes, wells, gardens and trees for Rs. 195 from Ram Chand in pargana Hisampur, sarkar Bahraich.[45] In 1677 Muhammad Arif purchased half the area of village Anchapur for Rs. 70 from one Dundi Shahi in Bahraich. The purchased area consisted of residential houses, gardens, tanks, wells and trees.[46] A document indicates that Shaikhs Nizamullah, Pir Muhammad and others, the proprietors (*maliks*) of the village Gondvi in pargana Hisampur, had mortgaged their village to one *madad-i-maash* holder Habibullah for Rs. 52.[47] These instances show that *madad-i-maah* holders also acted as revenue farmers and moneylenders. More importantly such activity clearly indicates that the grantees were more interested in investing their wealth in land occupations than in trade or business. They increased their means of income by occupying larger areas of land. Since in medieval India the landed classes were the dominating groups in society, the grantees of Awadh seem to have attempted to acquire the same position. It is important that the landed classes were not only dominant groups but were also politically powerful as suppliers of the largest part of state income to the royal authorities in form of land revenue. The acquisition of larger areas seems to have also aspired the grantees to make themselves politically strong. It needs to be mentioned that the expansion of landed properties was with the intention to increase income and enable a grantee to register as an active member of the agrarian class. Grantees never prepared to surrender the *madad-i-maash* grants which they were given to earn their livelihood. They retained their grants despite being financially well off.[48] Such privileges particularly in the eighteenth century enabled the grantees to acquire a share in the surplus of the area.

The grantees were not authorised to exercise *milkiyat* rights over their *madad-i-maash* grants. As a rule, these were assigned to them as loans (*ariyat*). However, in latter half of the seventeenth century the grantees of Awadh began to ignore the rule. Those who held large areas of grants freely leased out and sold their lands. In 1678, one Parwa Sahi had taken some *madad-i-maash* lands on lease for Rs. 49 in village Naukana, sarkar Bahraich.[49] In 1698 Muhammad Arif leased out some *madad-i-maash* lands for Rs. 105 in village Panyanhari, pargana Haveli Bahraich for three years.[50] In 1704 Shah Muhammad leased out his 2 *bighas madad-i-maash* lands in pargana Sandila, sarkar Lucknow. These instances point to the emergence of proprietary rights (*milkiyat*) in *madad-i-maash* lands. It is significant that the state did not attempt to enforce the original rules on *madad-i-maash* holders. It seems that the grantees of the suba had considerable influence at the local level and were well connected with royal court. The conversion of *madad-i-massh* land from *ariyat* to *milkiyat* clearly indicates that the grantees' power increased to the extent that they used the *madad-i-maash* grants according to their convenience. Generally *madad-i-maash* lands were less fertile. Once the grantees could sell and lease them out they could purchase lands in fertile areas. It is evident that some grantees of the suba were selling and leasing out their *madad-i-maash* grants, and were purchasing the lands of others.[51] Thus it can be assumed that the grantees of Awadh acquired considerable power in the socio-economic life of the suba in late seventeenth century. They continued their attempts to get more privileges and political importance by acquiring proprietary rights over their *madad-i-maash* grants in following century.

For the management of *madad-i-maash* grants, the state had established a separate department. This department was managed by officials who were expected to implement the law and state regulations and keep the grantees in control.[52] However, in Awadh the state officials were not capable of enforcing the prescribed rules and regulations. It is evident that despite the acquisition of *zamindari* rights by the grantees of Awadh they were exempted from cesses. When any particular official attempted to levy cesses on wealthy grantees, he faced their opposition, and ultimately had to refund the collected amount to the grantees.[53] Moreover in some areas even the appointment and dismissal of the *mutawallis* of the pargana depended largely on the will of the grantees. The jobs of the former were secure so long as they worked in the interest of the grantees.[54]

Our analysis thus shows that the *madad-i-maash* holders of Awadh acquired unusual power in the late seventeenth century onwards. They were not merely the members of a class which depended solely on the state for its existence, but in practice this class had been one of the major surplus appropriators of the suba. Being of the religious calling they received considerable importance in society. Moreover, they got many perquisites in lieu of performing religious rituals at different occasions. Since some *madad-i-maash* holders also held the religio-judicial offices that were hereditary, they accumulated enough wealth and gathered large followings. Many *madad-i-maash* holders increased their sources of income by purchasing *zamindari* rights of the areas in addition to their *madad-i-maash* lands. On the other hand they also enjoyed the benefit of *madad-i-maash* grants on the same grounds as their ancestors. The most important change took place in the position of *madad-i-maash* holders of Awadh was the acquisition of *milkiyat* by the grantees over their grants. They now acted as revenue farmer and money lenders in the suba. In the eighteenth century they were not just members of *lashkar-i-duagon* (army of prayers) but had become active members of the landed aristocracy. On the whole persons of a parasitic class had now become members of a strong social group of the suba.

All this created new social tensions. *Madad-i-maash* holders prior to second half of the seventeenth century were recognized as a group who was expected to devote its whole time in religious activities and for the welfare of the people. But when after 1700 in Awadh they turned into an exploiting group, the other powerful social groups particularly zamindars became suspicious and land wars between the grantees and zamindars of the suba became inevitable.

NOTES

1. M.A. Ansari, *Administrative Documents,* Doc. Nos. 2, 3, 37 and 38.
2. A.L. Srivastava, *Akbar the Great,* vol. I, Agra, 1962, pp. 125–6. It is important to note Akbar became an staunch follower of Shaikh Salim Chisti when with his grace a son was born to his wife. He named his son Salim. Even after the death of Salim Chisti in 1570 Akbar gave great importance to the Shaikh's family. The sons and sons-in-laws of Salim Chisti were assigned public offices by the emperor. Afzal Husain, 'The Family of Shaikh Salim Chisti during the reign of Jahangir', *Medieval India: A Miscellany,* vol. II, pp. 61–2.
3. Yusuf Husain, *Glimpses of Medieval Indian Culture,* p. 59. 'Aurangzeb wanted to give a grant of land to Shah Abdur Rahim, a divine and mystic but the Shah

Saheb declined to accept this offer as he did not like to have any connection with the court', ibid., p. 59.

4. See the chapter, 'Concentration and Dispersal'.
5. Irfan Habib, *Agrarian System of Mughal India,* Bombay, 1963 p. 304.
6. Ibid.
7. The scholars of the pargana Bilgram were famous for their learning. They imparted education in different parts of the country. The educational activities of Firangi Mahal *madrasa* of Lucknow also were famous over the country and even in some foreign countries. See Chapter 5.
8. See Chapter 5.
9. It may be mentioned that the social activities of *madad-i-maash* holders brought considerable political patronage to them. For instance the educational activities of Mulla Qutub-ud-Din of pargana Sihali, sarkar Lucknow were greatly appreciated by the Mughal state. From Akbar's reign to through the eighteenth century the family of Mulla Qutub-ud-Din received support from the Mughal government. It is important to note that when Aurangzeb was informed that Mulla Qutub-ud-Din had been killed by the zamindars of Sihali, he was shocked. He not only ordered the governor of the suba to kill the executors of Mulla Qutub-ud-Din, but he also made new arrangement for the settlement of Mulla's family in pargana Haveli Lucknow so that the family could live safely and could impart education. M.R. Ansari, *Bani-i-Dars-i-Nizami*, pp. 27–30.
10. Allahabad Doc. No. 254.
11. In Islam the interpretation of religious laws is not a monopoly of any particular class or group of society, but since in medieval India the Koran was not translated into regional languages people depended on the *ulema* for interpretation of the religious codes.
12. C.A. Elliot, *The Chronicle of Oanao*, Allahabad, 1862, p. 115.
13. Brahmans, the highest caste of four varnas and recipients of all privileges might have reacted if the Sufis tried to interfere in their established religious practices.
14. 'The *Sufi* practices soon entered into silent compromise with popular Hinduism and the worship of saints dead and alive, the reverence paid to tomb and relics, the believe in the efficacy of the intervention of the saints in the winning of a cherished things or retarding an expected evil coupled with pantheistic ideas borrowed from Hinduism brought Islam near the stage where syncretism was possible'. Sheikh Abdur Rashid, *History of Indo-Pakistan Subcontinent* (*1707–1806*), vol. I, Lahore, 1978, p. 4.
15. H.R. Nevill, *District Gazetteer Faizabad*, p. 260.
16. Allahabad Doc. Nos. 3, 7, 8, 11, 73, 168, 169, 204, 764, 805, 833, 839, 857, 1190; NAI, 1248, 1297, 1740, 2171, 2578/13.
17. According to N.A. Siddiqui, 'The local public opinion in Mughal period took the form of *Mahzarana* or memorandum, signed by a large number of *Shurafa*, especially Shaikhs and Sayyids which was sent to the court. The local public opinion of Shurafa assumed considerable importance when the central authority instituted an enquiry between the two different officials of the state.'

'Pulls and Preassures on the Faujdar Under the Mughals', PIHC, 1967, Pt. I, pp. 243–4.

18. In medieval India prominent religious duties were performed by persons of the Shaikh and Sayyid groups. Therefore, they were recognized as pious class of Muslim community as according to varna system Brahmans were highest caste and priest class in Hindu community.
19. *Muftis* were interpreter of Islamic laws.
20. Irfan Habib, *Agrarian System*, p. 311.
21. Muzaffar Alam, 'Some Aspects', PIHC, 1974, p. 201.
22. Shaikh Ghulam Husain, *Sharaif-i-Usmani* (a biographical dictionary of important families of Bilgram compiled in middle of the eighteenth century), Dept. of History, AMU, Aligarh, p. 70. Compare Muzaffar Alam, 'Some Aspects', PIHC, 1974, p. 201.
23. Ibid.
24. Allahabad Doc. Nos. 836, 838, 882, 934 and 1280.
25. Ibid., No. 55.
26. Compare Muzaffar Alam, 'Some Aspects', PIHC, 1974, p. 201.
27. Shireen Moosvi, '*Sayurghal* Statistics', *IHR*, 1979, no. 2, pp. 282–9.
28. Ibid.
29. Allahabad Doc. No. 55.
30. Ibid., No. 1190.
31. Ibid., No. 1196.
32. Ibid., No. 1189.
33. Ibid., Nos. 824, 1216, 1219, 1221 and 1224.
34. Iqbal Husain, 'Calendar of Khairabad Documents', *Islamic Culture*, 1979, no. 1, p. 48.
35. Compare Muzaffar Alam, 'Some Aspects', PIHC, 1974, p. 199.
36. An ordinary zamindar was expected to render some services to the state. Whenever, a *madad-i-maash* holder, despite acquiring *zamindari* rights was free from all obligations.
37. Allahabad Doc. No. 1283.
38. Ibid., No. 1309.
39. *Satrahi* was the technical term of he *zamindari* right, used in Awadh.
40. Allahabad Doc. No. 439 and 457.
41. Iqbal Husain, 'Calendar of Khairabad Documents', *Islamic Culture*, 1979, No. 1, p. 48.
42. Compare, Satish Chandra, *Parties and Politics at Mughal Court 1704–1740*, Delhi, 1972, p. xxvi.
43. Allahabad Doc. 1285.
44. Compare, Muzaffar Alam, 'Some Aspects', PIHC, 1974, p. 200.
45. Allahabad Doc. No. 1194. In the same year Mir Sayyid Ahmed purchased 1/3 part of village Pansajat for Rs. 405 from Dasi and Laxman in pargana Hisampur, ibid., No. 1196.
46. Ibid., No. 1189.

47. Ibid., No. 1317.
48. Compare Muzaffar Alam, 'Some Aspects', PIHC, 1974, p. 200. In 1678–9 qanungo of pargana Haveli Bahraich realized the Qanugo Mir Sayyid Ahmed and other grantees. However, the qanungo was ordered by the state to return the collected amount of 'illegal cess' to the grantees. Allahabad Doc. No. 1291. It is important to note that the said Sayyid had acquired *zamindari* rights in 1672, Ibid., No. 1196. Therefore, it seems that qanungo might have understood Sayyid Ahmed capable of paying cesses because of his sound economic condition. Moreover, the grantees were given exemption from the cesses on the condition that they had no other means of their livelihood except the assigned lands. But as the grantees had arranged other sources of income, qanungo might have also thought that the said grantee did not deserve for the exemption from cesses. Compare, Muzaffar Alam, 'Some Aspects', PIHC, 1974, p. 205.
49. Allahabad Doc. No. 1230. In 1699 Muhammad Arif leased out some *madad-i-maash* lands to Muhammad Abid for Rs. 75 in pargana Haveli Bahraich for four years. Ibid., No. 1231.
50. Ibid. No. 439. In 1672 Shaikh Jarullah, *aimmadar* of village Mahasona, pargana Sandila sold his *madad-i-maash* lands to one Ruhul Amin Chaudhary for Rs. 1,714. Ibid., No. 292.
51. Ibid., Nos. 1189, 1230 and 1231.
52. The department for the administration of grant lands was headed by the *sadr-us-sudur* at centre. In the province it was run by the *sadr-i-juz* and the *mutawallis* and several other officials such as *qazis, muftis* and *qanungoes*, etc. The *sadr-i-juz* was the head of *madad-i-maash* institution at suba level and *mutawallis* run the administration of this institution, in the pargana. The *qazis, muftis* and qanungos settled the disputed case regarding the grants. All these offices were under the control of the central authority. Compare Muzaffar Alam, 'Some Aspects', PIHC, 1974, p. 200. For the study of Administration of *madad-i-maash* institutions in detail, see Ibn Hasan, *Central Structure of Mughal Empire*, Delhi, 1970, pp. 255–88. N.A. Siddiqui, *Land Revenue Administration Under the Mughals (1700–1750)*, Bombay, 1970, pp. 128–31.
53. Allahabad Doc. No. 1212.
54. Compare Muzaffar Alam, 'Some Aspects', PIHC, 1974, p. 221.

CHAPTER 7

Relations among the Grantees

THE MUTUAL RELATIONS OF THE GRANTEES

The *madad-i-maash* holders were a group, but economically they differed greatly among themselves. In Awadh there were many *madad-i-maash* holders who held sizeable lands and accumulated huge wealth, plus many with small holdings and no great affluence. Contrasts in wealth meant that their mutual relations also varied. Every *madad-i-maash* holder of the suba tried to protect his own individual interest instead of that of the group as a whole.

In Awadh, during second half of the seventeenth century, the *madad-i-maash* holders began to expand the area of their grant lands and therefore, their mutual relations became strained. Those who also held public office started taking undue advantage of their position, illegally occupying the grants of unconditional grant holders. Qazi Wali Muhammad came into conflict with the grantees of parganas Sailak, Fakhrpur and Hisampur, sarkar Bahraich during Aurangzeb's reign.[1] The cause of conflict between the grantees and Qazi Wali Muhammad was the illegal occupation of grant lands by the latter.[2] It may be mentioned that the entire family of the said *qazi* forcibly occupied *madad-i-maash* lands of others. His relatives followed suit.[3]

The attempts of the grantees to increase the area of their *madad-i-maash* lands also created strained relations between co-sharers. *Madad-i-maash* holders of the same family fought with each other. In 1674 Sayyid Taj Muhammad struggled with his co-sharer Abdul Rasul on the division of *madad-i-maash* grants in pargana Hisampur, sarkar Bahraich.[4] The conflict between them continued for ten years. Ultimately in 1684 Taj Muhammad was killed by Abdul Rasul.[5] There are some other instances regarding the conflict among the co-sharers of *madad-i-maash* grants.[6] Generally such conflicts occurred due to forcible occupation of *madad-i-maash* grants of others by a particular co-share.

Beside conflicts between conditional and unconditional grant holders and among co-sharers, some *madad-i-maash* holders clashed when they tried extend their *madad-i-maash* holdings by encroaching on those of others. When a powerful grantee found that a grantee was in trouble due to certain reasons, the former started to encroach on his *madad-i-maash* lands. In 1669 Shaikh Sibghatullah illegally occupied 250 *bighas* of *madad-i-maash* lands in pargana Bilgram, sarkar Lucknow.[7]

In 1742 Bahauddin, a grantee of pargana Mallawan, sarkar Lucknow, left his town. Taking advantage of his absence, Sayyid Farhatullah, another grantee of the same pargana, forcibly seized his *madad-i-maash* lands and house, *purah*, and gardens.[8] The family of Bahauddin protested and made representation against Farhatullah without any result. The dispute between them continued for decades.

The internal feuds of the grantees of the suba indicate that in the late seventeenth century and in the next century there seems to have been a race to illegally occupy lands of the weaker grantees and establish undisputed authority there. It is evident that conflicts among elite *madad-i-maash* holders were especially frequent. Those *madad-i-maash* holders who were involved in conflict were economically well off and socially influential. The conflicts between Qazi Wali Muhammad and Sayyid Muhammad Arif, Sayyid Ahmed and Ghayasuddin of sarkar Bahraich illustrate the point.[9] It seems that the desire to establish one's influence in the area led to strained relations with others. The grantees of the lower class however hardly could acquire the *madad-i-maash* lands of others or bear the strain of such conflict. In such conflicts among the grantees of the upper class, large sums of money were spent. Mostly these disputes were settled with the intervention of the state.[10] Thus it can be assumed that the mutual relations of the grantees were strained. However, such conflicts were common among the elites.

Though the grantees of the suba fought with each other, it is important to note that they became united whenever any other social group attempted to create problems for them. When local officials collected illegal cesses from them, all grantees of the area made representations against them. In most of the cases the decision of the state was in their favour.[11] This indicates that the grantees of the suba were conscious to maintain a respectable position for their own group and this gave all grantees a sense of security. Within their own group however the grantees more individualistic, every grantee was interested in strengthening his own position and mutual relations were not cordial. Unity was maintained only against external pressure. Such unity led to the emergence of a powerful social group of *madad-i-maash* holders in Awadh after 1700.

RELATIONS WITH THE ZAMINDARS

Towards the end of the seventeenth-century relations with the zamindars of Awadh seem to have become strained. The attempts of the grantees to acquire local power affected the position of the zamindars. There are many cases of hostility of zamindars against the local grantees.

It has been mentioned that in late in the seventeenth century *madad-i-maash* holders of the suba began to acquire *zamindari* rights.[12] The zamindars began to check the increasing power of the grantees, and to adopt a hostile attitude towards the latter. The zamindars of pargana Harha, sarkar Lucknow harassed the Sayyid grantees of the pargana badly.[13] In last years of Aurangzeb's reign Rustam Khan, Nasir Khan, Fatheshah, Man Singh, Nayan Rai and Kharak Rai, the zamindars of pargana Sidhora compelled the grantees of Zaidpur of the pargana to pay certain illegal cesses.[14]

There are many instances when increasing power of the grantees not only led to the creation of strained relations with zamindars but also to the disturbing of the law and order of the villages. Many *aimma* villages were attacked by the latter. In 1716 Sayyid *madad-i-mash* holders of village Ahrora, pargana Hisampur, sarkar Baḥraich petitioned that Sukha, Bachchu, Udai Singh, Balla, Gajja, Bhula Makand the Rajput zamindars invaded the said *aimma* village. These zamindars murdered Sayyids Karam Ali, Ibrahim, and Shaikh Sajjan; five women were burnt; and survivors were expelled from the village. The zamindars demolished all houses of the *aimmadars*, and occupied their *madad-i-maash* lands.[15] Similarly, the village of Badholia, Kamelpur, Kauhatta and Malhari which were under the control of Sayyids were completely devasted, the graveyards of their ancestors, and the mosques and *madrasas* demolished.[2]

It is important to note that where the *madad-i-maash* holders were in conflict with the zamindars, it was difficult for the former to utilize their assigned lands. Even the state failed to make any lasting settlement between the grantees and the zamindars. The only alternative before the state (to save the grantees from oppression from zamindars) was to transfer the *madad-i-maash* lands of the grantees to other places. In 1667, 500 *bighas* of *madad-i-maash* lands of Shaikh Izzatullah was transferred in pargana Haveli Lucknow because the grantee had poor relations with the zamindars of that area.[17] In 1679 the grant of Shaikh Abul Faiz was transferred in sarkar Khairabad due to the hostility of zamindars.[18] In 1691, Aurangzeb transferred the family of Mulla Qutub-ud-Din from pargana Sahali to Lucknow because of the enmity of the zamindars with the family.[19] There are many other instances which indicate that owing to the hostility of the zamindars the *madad-i-maash* holders of some places of Awadh had to face great hardship. It may be mentioned that generally the Rajput zamindars of the suba were hostile to *madad-i-maash* holders.[20]

Such conflicts between the grantees and zamindars have been described as communal wars in a recent study.[21] However, this needs reconsideration. The conflicts between the grantees and the zamindars can be interpreted in terms of class war. At the places where the conflicts between these groups occurred, hardly any reference is found that the people of the different classes of that area formed separate groups on the basis of religion and fought wars on religious grounds. On the contrary references are available that Hindu and Muslim zamindars jointly attacked Muslim *madad-i-maash* holders. In the last years of Aurangzeb's reign the zamindars who harassed the Sayyid *madad-i-maash* holders included three, Nazir Khan, Rustam and Haisham Khan, Muslims.[22] More significantly pargana Sidhora consisted of large number of Muslim zamindars,[23] but the zamindars did not help the Sayyid *madad-i-maash* holders of the pargana against the Hindu zamindars.

There are many references to cordial relations between the people of both Hindu and Muslim communities. It is known that Mohan Singh a recalcitrant zamindar of Tiloi around 1700 was a staunch follower of the Sufi Saint Shah Ashraf Jahangir. Mohan Singh used to say with pride that his *zamindari* had the blessing of the saint.[24] It is important to note that the controllers of the shrine of the Sufi were assigned *madad-i-maash* grants in sarkars of Lucknow and Awadh.[25] There are also some instance regarding the support of Rajput zamindars to Muslim *madad-i-maash* holders. During Aurangzeb's reign, Wali Muhammad, the *qazi* and *madad-i-maash* holder of pargana Hisampur, sarkar Bahraich illegally occupied the lands of Mir Sayyid Ahmed and Muhammad Arif. The *qazi* was supported by Ram Singh, a zamindar of the same sarkar who had enmity with Sayyid Ahmed and Muhammad Arif.[26] It is important to note that that these two Sayyids were purchasing *zamindari* rights very rapidly in the sarkar of Bahraich and had considerable influence in the area.[27] It seems that the increasing power of the aforesaid grantees clashed with the interests of the zamindar of the area, therefore, the above-mentioned zamindar helped the enemies of the former. So that he could decrease the influence of the grantees-cum-zamindars.

The class war between the grantees and the zamindar is further illustrated by the fact that Muslim zamindars also came into conflict with the Muslim *madad-i-maash* holders. In 1691, Mulla Qutub-ud-Din, a *madad-i-maash* holder of pargana Sahali, sarkar Lucknow, was killed by the Muslim zamindars of the pargana Sahali, Bijnore, Fatehpur.[28] There are instance in which Hindu zamindars and Muslim grantees made transactions with each other in terms of setting and leasing out their lands. In 1672 and 1677 Mir Sayyid Ahmed and Muhammad Arif, two *madad-i-maash* holders purchased lands from Ram Chand and Dundi, in pargana Hisampur and Bahraich respectively.[29] In 1678 one Parwa Sahi had taken *madad-i-maash* lands on lease from one Muslim grantee in pargana Bahraich.[30]

Apart from the such instances, it also deserves to be mentioned that a large number of state officials in Awadh were Hindus and had direct contact with the Muslim *madad-i-maash* holders.[31] But these *madad-i-maash* holders had no enmity with the officials. More importantly some grant documents bear the signature of officials in Hindi.[32] But no objection was made by the grantees. This clearly indicates that there was no religious conflicts between Muslim *madad-i-maash* holders and Hindu zamindars of the suba. If there would have been any communal crisis the people of different communities of Awadh might have formed their own separate factions on religious grounds. It may be mentioned that in Awadh the majority of the parganas consisted of Hindu zamindars,[33] but hardly any example is found regarding the formation of a religious body operating against a particular community. More importantly Hindu zamindars of the suba had no enmity with those Muslim grantees who were not endangering their position.

Thus it can be assumed that conflicts between the *madad-i-maash* holders and zamindars of the suba occurred because of the former's increasing power at local level. The grantees by acquiring *zamindari* rights hampered the interests of the zamindars economically as well as socially. Since the grantees acquired *zamindari* rights of a particular area, the zamindars of that area were deprived of their *nankar* and *rusum-i-zamindari*. It was customary that the zamindars participated in social functions of their areas and for it they were given honour by the people. As some areas of *zamindari* lands were occupied by the grantees, the scope of social influence of the *zamindari* became narrow. Therefore, to save their economic decline and maintain their social influence the zamindars of the suba attacked the grant holders. It is wrong to assume that conflicts between Muslim *madad-i-maash* holders and Hindu zamindars were based on religious grounds. These conflicts can be interpreted in terms of class conflicts and not as communal conflicts.[34] However, these conflicts indicate that the grantees became a source of social disturbances at village level. The grantees, who were expected to maintain society peaceful, proved to be creator of problems in the society in eighteenth-century Awadh.

MADAD-I-MAASH HOLDERS RELATIONS WITH THE PROVINCIAL AND LOCAL OFFICIALS

Saadat Khan, first nawab of Awadh, adopted strict attitude towards the grantees of the suba.[35] He adopted the policy of resumption of grant lands and levying cesses on the grantees. Consequently he came into conflict with some powerful *madad-i-maash* holders of the suba.[36] However, his policy of resumption and assessment of grants was implemented only on those grantees who were economically well off. The majority of *madad-i-maash* holders of Awadh were free from the policy of the nawab. This can be ascertained from the fact that except the grantees of pargana Bilgram, no grantees of any other pargana protested against the nawab's policy. Moreover during the period of Nawab Saadat Khan the renewal and confirmation of grants were made as usually as in earlier period.[37] The relations of *madad-i-maash* holders on the whole were cordial.

During the periods of Safdarjang and Shuja-ud-Daula, the grantees of the suba were not subjected to any aggressive measure. They were treated well. It is evident that in eighteenth century a number of *madad-i-maash* holders of the suba acquired *zamindari* rights.[38] But hardly any measure was taken by the nawabs of Awadh to check such unlawful activities. The *madad-i-maash* lands of the grantees seem to have been treated as *zamindari* and *milkiyat* of the latter and not *ariyat*.[39] In 1740 the grant of an old pond was confirmed to the *qazi* of pargana as his proprietery right *malikana*.[40] A *madad-i-maash* document of 1745 describes *madad-i-mash* grant and *milkiyat* interchangeably.[41] Such concessions to the grantees show that relations between *madad-i-maash* holders and provincial official of Awadh were cordial.

As far as the grantees' relations with local officials were concerned, it seems that from the second half of the seventeenth century onwards grantees and local officials started influencing each other. Therefore, their relations became strained. The grantees were asked by the local officials to get their grants renewed and confirmed many times.[42] It became difficult for the grantees to satisfy the local officials at the time of the confirmation of the grants,[43] and so they proceeded to the royal court to get their grievances redressed. Such conflicts between the grantees and local officials seem to have disturbed law and order of the area. Because on one side the grantees were not in good terms with the zamindars, on the other, they also had conflict with the local officials.

RELATIONS WITH THE CENTRAL AUTHORITY

It is well established that the *madad-i-maash* holders were the creation of the central authority. Their privileges depend on the will of the emperor. It is evident that throughout the Mughal period, the emperor never imposed any burden on the grantees. In Awadh the grantees were given considerable importance by the central authority. This shows that the grantees of the suba had good relations with the central authority. In fact some grantees were so well connected with Mughal court that the grantees of pargana Bilgram defied the authority of Nawab Saadat Khan. Ultimately they received a favourable decision from the Emperor Muhammad Shah against the policy of the nawab.[44] It may be mentioned that the nawab who acted as deputy of Mughal emperor and controlled the whole suba had to make a compromise with the grantees.[45]

In the eighteenth century the relations between the zamindars and state authority had become strained. The state received a great resistance from zamindars of the suba. At this juncture grantees did not attempt to be disloyal to the state authority. Though they occupied *zamindari* right at several places, this right was acquired with the consent of the state, not by rebellion.[46] This shows that when grantees emerged as a strong landed force they remained dependent on the state for retaining their privileges and position at local level. It is important to mention that the grantees had no hope to get the support of zamindars and other rural elites, because their highly sound economic condition was not liked by the latter. In this way state was the sole protector of the interest of the grantees of the suba. Similarly, the state also depended on the grantees for social support at the local level. Since the zamindars of whole suba had become rebellious. The state hardly could be sure of their attitudes.

Moreover, a number of regional powers had emerged and the central authority hardly could be sure about the loyalty of the nawabs of the suba. Consequently, *madad-i-maash* holders were the most confident informer of the stability of the law and order in the suba.[47]

Therefore, the central authority adopted a generous policy towards grant holders.

The relations of the *madad-i-maash* holders with the different authorities of the suba shows that the grantees had no cordial relation with the zamindars and local officials. Since in eighteenth century the *madad-i-maash* holders of Awadh made rapid progress in terms of occupying sizeable lands, acquiring of *zamindari* and *milkiyat* rights, the zamindars, an ancestral landed aristrocratic class, seem to have taken the former's emergence as landed elites as threat to their position. Therefore, both the grantees and the zamindar became hostile to each other. Nevertheless, the grantees succeeded in maintaining good relations with the state. They intensified the process of acquiring *zamindaris* areas. However, neither provincial nor central authority could protect the grantees against the oppression of the zamindars. Since the zamindars were more powerful militarily as well as economically, grantees could hardly be successful in making substantial headway against the former. Consequently state favour to the grantees proved to be dangerous for the Mughal government itself. The local level the state authorities had continuous problems of the conflict between zamindars and grantees. Ultimately such conflicts led to the breakdown of the state control in rural areas.

NOTES

1. In 1672 Qazi Wali Muhammad forcibly occupied 5,375 *bighas* of *madad-i-maash* lands in pargana Hisampur. Allahabad Doc. No. 786. In 1676 he again illegally occupied a large size of *madad-i-maash* lands of Sayyid Ahmed, Muhammad Arif and Ghayasuddin in pargana Fakhrpur. Ibid. No. 1212. In 1679 he made another illegal occupation of 1,000 *bighas* of *madad-i-maash* lands in pargana Fakhrpur. Ibid., No. 1203.
2. Allahabad Doc. Nos. 786, 1203 and 1212
3. In 1679 Sayyid Jaffar, a relation of Qazi Wali Muhammad, illegally occupied the *madad-i-maash* land of the grantees in pargana Sailak and Hisampur. Allahabad Doc. No. 1201. He with the said *qazi* harassed the grantees. Ibid., No. 1202. It may be mentioned that such attitute of the relations of *qazis* seems to have led to the formation of group of *madad-i-maash* holders which would have been acted as anti-*qazis*.
4. Ibid., No. 857.
5. Ibid., No. 785.

6. In 1666 Sayyid Usman illegally occupied the share of his co-sharer *madad-i-maash* holder Bibi Lazyat in pargana Hisampur, sarkar Bahraich. Allahabad Doc. No. 1189. In 1722 Muhammad Rafi attempted to seize the *madad-i-maash* grant of his brother Muhammad Faruq in pargana Bilgram, sarkar Lucknow, Ibid., No. 41.
7. Ibid., No. 204.
8. Ibid., Nos. 44 and 46.
9. The position of these *madad-i-maash* holders can be estimated that they had sizeable lands. Ibid., Nos. 781, 803 and 1203. Sayyid Ahmed and Muhammad Arif were not simply *madad-i-maash* holders, but they exercised their power as zamindar of the area. Ibid., Nos. 1196, 1216, 1219 and 1222. The influence of Qazi Wali Muhammad can be judged from the fact that when in 1679 the state sent an army to put off his illegal activities he gathered a large number of miscreants and came into conflict with the state army. Ibid., No. 1202.
10. Ibid., Nos. 41, 204, 1189 and 1202.
11. In 1690 Haji Habibullah, an *amil*, forcibly occupied the *madad-i-maash* lands of one Shamsher in pargana Sandila, Sarkar Lucknow. All *aimmadars* of the pargana protested against the *amil* and filed a petition in the court of Nawab Diler Khan requesting him to restore the grant to the grantees. NAI 1486, 1546. In 1765 all *aimmadars* of pargana Amethi, sarkar Lucknow made a petition to the state against the collection of illegal cesses by one official. Allahabad Doc. No. 270.
12. See Chapter 6.
13. Compare Muzaffar Alam, 'Some Aspects', PIHC, 1974, p. 202.
14. Allahabad Doc. No. 1565.
15. Ibid., No. 1236.
16. Compare Muzaffar Alam, 'Some Aspects', PIHC, 1974, p. 202.
17. Allahabad Doc. Nos. 1190, 1–2.
18. Ibid., No. 1212.
19. M.R. Ansari, *Bani-i-Dars-i-Nizami*, pp. 21–30.
20. In the early eighteenth century (after the death of Aurangzeb) the Gaur zamindars compelled the grantees of sarkar Khairabad to migrate from their native place to the neighbouring territories of Bangash Afghans of Farrukhabad. These grantees failed to settle anywhere for twelve years. They wandered homeless. Subsequently when Safdarjang became the nawab of Awadh he made a compromise with the Gaur zamindars of Khairabad. At the same time the above-mentioned grantees were restored their houses and other properties in Khariabad. Munshi Sahib Rai, *Khujista-i-Kalam*, Rotograph, Raghubir Singh Collection, Sitamau (a collection of letters of Nawab Muhammad Khan Bangash), pp. 165–6. Compare Muzaffar Alam, 'Some Aspects', PIHC, 1974, pp. 202–3, 206. The Sukha (Singha) of some villages in pargana Kheri and Laharpur, sarkar Khairabad caused ruin to the families of these pargana. Shiv Das Lakhnavi, *Shahnama-i-Munawwar Kalam*, English trans. by Syed Hasan Askari, Patna, 1982, pp 126–8. The zamindars of pargana Daryabad attacked the grantees of the area. *Ajaib-ul-Afaq* (a collection of letters of Chhabela Ram, Girdhar Lal and some Akhbarat

of Farrukh Siyar's reign), Rotagraph, Raghubir Singh Collection, Sitamau, p. 206. Compare, Muzaffar Alam, 'Some Aspects', PIHC, 1974, p. 206. *Insha-i-Roshan Kalam* of Bhupat Rai records several conflicts between the grantees and the zamindars of the suba. Kanpur, 1298 A.H., pp. 3–6, 14, 27. Compare Muzaffar Alam, 'Some Aspects', PIHC, 1974, pp. 202, 205.

21. C.A. Bayly, 'The Pre-History of Communalism, Religious conflicts of India, 1700–1860', *Modern Asian Studies,* vol. 19, pt. 2, April 1985, New York, pp. 191–2.
22. Allahabad Doc. No. 1565.
23. *Ain.*, vol. I (English trans.), p. 189.
24. Compare Muzaffar Alam, 'Some Aspects', PIHC, 1974, p. 206.
25. Rafat Bilgrami, 'Some Mughal Revenue Grants', *Medieval India: A Miscellany,* vol. II, pp. 309–21.
26. Allahabad Doc. No. 934.
27. Ibid. Nos. 1196, 1216, 1219, 1221 and 1222.
28. M.R. Ansari, *Bani-i-Dars-Nizami,* p. 21.
29. Allahabad Doc. Nos. 1194, 1189 and 1196.
30. Ibid., No. 892.
31. Ibid., Nos. 878, 880, 882.
32. Ibid., Nos. 880, 881 and 883.
33. *Ain.*, vol. I (English trans.), pp. 184–6.
34. Compare Muzaffar Alam, 'Some Aspects', PIHC, 1974, p. 202.
35. Ghulam Ali Azad Bilgrami, *Maathir-ul-Kiram,* vol. I, Lahore, 1971, p. 222. Compare Muzaffar Alam, *The Crisis of Empire in Mughal North India: Awadh and the Punjab 1707–1748,* Delhi, 1986, p. 220.
36. For example the faujdar and diwan of pargana Bilgram faced great resistance from the *madad-i-maash* holders of the pargana. Under the leadership of the *qazi* of the pargana, they continued their resistance for seven years. Subsequently with the help of the emperor the *qazi* succeeded in forcing the nawab to withdraw his aggressive policy towards the grantees. Compare Muzaffar Alam, *The Crisis of Empire,* p. 220.
37. NAI, 1391, 1378, 1582, Allahabad Doc. No. 11.
38. In the entire region from pargana Kakori, sarkar Lucknow to the border of suba of Allahabad a number of Shaikh, Shaikhzadas and Sayyids had their *zamindaris.* The ancestors of all these zamindars were *madad-i-maash* holders prior to 1700. S.A.A. Rizvi, *Shah Waliullah and His Times,* Canberra, 1980, pp. 183–4.
39. *Madad-i-maash* grantees were assigned the lands as loans (*ariyat*). They were not expected to exercise proprietery rights. Even after 1690 when Aurangzeb made the grants completely hereditary it was insisted to treat the grants as something held on loan. Irfan Habib, *Agrarian System of Mughal India,* Bombay, 1963, pp. 303–4, 306.
40. Muzaffar Alam, *The Crisis of Empire,* p. 223.
41. Ibid., p. 247.
42. Allahabad Doc. Nos. 767, 779, 778 and 834.

43. M.A. Ansari (ed.), *Administrative Documents of Mughal India*, Delhi, 1983, p. 4.
44. Compare Muzaffar Alam, *The Crisis of Empire*, p. 220.
45. Ibid., p. 243.
46. The official documents mention the grantees as zamindars and *malik*. This shows that the grantees status as zamindar was recognised by the Mughal government. Allahabad Doc. No. 1224.
47. It may be mentioned that some grantees of Awadh had direct contact with the royal court. For example the family of Mulla Nizam-ud-Din of Firangi Mahal in pargana and sarkar of Lucknow was well associated with the Mughal Emperors Aurangzeb and Muhammad Shah. M.R. Ansari, *Bani-Dars-i-Nizami*, pp. 23–86.

CHAPTER 8

Conclusion

The state considered it a duty to provide for the needy and the pious in ancient India and in the Sultanate period this practice continued in the form of assignments of revenue free land. However, in Mughal time some changes were made in the system and it was made more systematic. During this period revenue free grants were generally known as *madad-i-maash, sayurghal* or *aimma.* In Akbar's reign a definite policy was adopted in connection with such grants. The eligibility of the recipients of *madad-i-maash* grant was determined. It was decided that grants were to be assigned in both cultivated and waste-but-cultivable land. For the retention of such grants for long periods, the loyalty of the grantee to the state was the main consideration. This policy of the assignment of *madad-i-maash* lands continued through the Mughal period.

Broadly speaking, the following conclusions can be drawn from the present study. First, through the assignment of *madad-i-maash* grants, the state created a class at the lowest level of the administration set-up, expected complete loyalty in return. They were to pray for the endurance of the empire and watch the interests of the state in their respective regions.

The lands assigned in the *madad-i-maash* grants were both in cultivated area and in the waste-but-cultivable land. The assignees were expected to bring under plough the cultivable land making their entire assigned land cultivated. At the time of renewal, half of their assigned land was resumed and in its place a fresh half of waste-but-cultivable land was assigned. This practice was perhaps with two considerations:

(a) The quantum of assistance in terms of yield was initially determined on the basis of the two different kind of fertility of assigned land. But once the cultivable waste was converted into cultivated land the actual yield from the total land must have exceeded the stipulated return. Therefore, to retain the quantum of assistance the practice of resumption of cultivated land and assignment of waste-but-cultivable land must have continued.

(b) This practice would have provided a mechanism for expanding the size of the actual cultivated land of the empire, thus making the same available to the state for use as *khalsa* or *jagir* land.

Some changes were made in the nature of assignment of these grants in the second half of these grants in the second half of the seventeenth century. These grants were made hereditary with no reduction in size at the time of renewal. In the absence of a son, the grant was renewed in favour of relatives in the prescribed sequence.

Continuation of such grantees or their families in a particular area made them socially strong and motivated them politically to establish their authority at the local level. They acquired *zamindaris* and became restive, creating administrative problems.

It is difficult to believe that these grantees remained rural based. In the light of the present study it could be said that they were both urban and rural based due to a variety of reasons.

The grantees over a period of time emerged as an economically strong group. The grants which were initially assigned to them as maintenance increased manyfold either through additional grants or by illegal occupation of land.

The grantees did not remain confined to their socio-religious duties, they gradually developed an interest in trade, commerce and education. It provided them greater respectability in society and in turning them into an elite class.

The *madad-i-maash* grants were assigned to women also. This had not only provided them social recognition but also made them economically self-reliant and more actively associated with the socio-economic life of the area.

The assignment of *madad-i-maash* in different pargana of the suba varied from area to area. The statistics in the *Ain* indicate this variation from 0.41 per cent to 23.30 per cent in different parganas. The total assignment of such grants was 4.2 per cent of the total *jama* of the suba.

The *madad-i-maash* grantees gradually acquired proprietary rights (*milkiyat*) over their land, thus leading to the emergence of a new class of landed aristrocracy in the rural areas.

The emergence of the grantees as a class with a new socio-economic status not only created vested interests but led to socio-political tension at the regional level.

Through the present work an attempt has been made, perhaps for the first time, to study various aspects of the assignment of *madad-i-mash* during the Mughal period. The study of this important insitution of Mughal administrative set-up unfolded interesting information and details which may help in appreciating the impact of this system on socio-religious and political life at the local level.

APPENDIX I: PERCENTAGE OF *SAYURGHAL* IN THE SUBA OF AWADH*

The total *jama* of the suba of Awadh was 20,17,58,172 *dams* out of which 85,21,658 *dams* were assigned as *sayurghal* which comes to 4.2 per cent of total *jama.*

S. No.	*Pargana*	*Per cent of sayurghal of total jama*	*Zamindars*
		I. SARKAR OF AWADH	
1	Awadh	8.00	Brahman, Kumbi
2	Ambodh	0.56	Bais
3	Ibrahimabad	23.30	Ansari
4	Panchamrath	0.09	Rajputs
5	Bilhari	0.029	Bachgoti
6	Basodhi	0.30	Bachgoti
7	Thanah Badon	8.50	Bachgoti
8	Daryabad	4.22	Rajput, Chauhan, Bais
9	Sailak	4.25	Rajput, Raikwar
10	Sultanpur	2.60	Bachgoti
11	Satanpur	6.09	Bais (Islam) Bachgoti
12	Subeha	5.40	Rajput
13	Sarwapali	4.00	Bachgoti
14	Satrikh	8.23	Ansari
15	Gawarchak	0.10	Raikwar
16	Kishni	9.24	Rajput
17	Mangalsi	6.35	Sombansi
18	Naipur	0.10	Various
		II. SARKAR OF GORAKHPUR	
1	Utraula	0.50	Afghan-i-Miyanah
2	Unhaula	1.80	Bisen
3	Dewaparah and Katla	0.33	Bisen
4	Rihli	1.29	Rajput Bisen
5	Gorakhpur	0.70	Surajbansi
6	Maghar & Ratanpur	1.40	Bisen Bais

**Ain-i-Akbari*, vol. II (English trans.), pp. 184–90.

S. No.	Parganaa	Per cent of sayurghal of total jama	Zamindars
	III. SARKAR OF BAHRAICH		
1	Bahraich	4.40	Rajput
2	Ansarpur	0.34	Raikwar, Bisen
3	Fakhrpur	1.80	Raikwar
4	Firozabad	0.21	Rajput
5	Khararsa	0.19	Bais
	IV. SARKAR OF KHAIRABAD		
1	Baror Anjanah	2.48	Rajput, Brahman
2	Baswah	—	Rajput, Bachhal
3	Pati	2.50	Asnin
4	Baswan	2.30	Asnin
5	Chhatyapur	2.33	Rajput, Gaur
6	Khariabad, 2 Mahals	8.059	Brahman
7	Sandi	6.39	Sombansi
8	Sarah	0.41	Chauhan
9	Sadrpur	1.87	Janwar
10	Gopamau	9.99	Rajput, Gaur
11	Kheri	1.55	Bisen, Rajput, Janwar
12	Laharpur	7.00	Brahman
13	Machharhatta	0.16	Rajput and Buchar
14	Nimkhar	2.00	Ahir
15	Hargaraon	13.00	—
	V. SARKAR OF LUCKNOW		
1	Amethi	10.00	Ansari
2	Unam	12.60	Sayyid
3	Isauli	5.70	Rajput, Bachgot
4	Asiyun	7.63	Bais, Chandel
5	Bilgram	7.00	Sayyid, Bais
6	Bangarman	4.00	Rajput, Ghelot
7	Bijnor	7.70	Chauhan
8	Bari	4.00	Bais
9	Pangwan	3.00	Bais
10	Betholi	2.40	Rajput, Jat
11	Jahalotar	2.00	Rajput
12	Dewi	9.00	Bais, Brahman
13	Ranbarpur	3.00	Ghelot, Bach

S. No.	Parganaa	Per cent of sayurghal of total jama	Zamindars
14	Sandilah	8.00	Rajput, Chandel
15	Saipur	1.00	Chandel, Rajput
16	Sarosi	0.13	Bais, Brahman
17	Satanpur	1.00	—
18	Sahali	19.00	Rajput
19	Sidhor	18.00	Afghan, Rajput
20	Sandi	3.50	Rajput
21	Saron	1.40	Rajput, Shaikhzadas
22	Fatehpur	8.00	Kumbi, Rajput
23	Fatehpur Chaurasi	1.00	Rajput
24	Kursi	4.00	Rajput
25	Kakori	1.20	Rajput, Bisen
26	Kachhandan	1.00	Chandel
27	Lucknow	14.00	Shaikhzadas, Brahman, Kayasth
28	Malihabad	2.40	Bais
29	Mallawan	6.16	Bais
30	Mohan	10.00	Bais, Rajput
31	Moraon	0.28	Rajput, Bais
32	Madiaon	3.00	Barkhala (Rajput)
33	Mohanah	0.90	Rajput
34	Manawi	2.00	Musalman, Rajput
35	Makraed	1.00	Rajput
36	Harha	0.26	Rajput, Bais
37	Hardoi	2.00	Brahman

APPENDIX II: SOME GRANTEES OF THE SUBA AND THE SIZES OF THEIR HOLDINGS

S. No.	*Name of the grantee*	*Year*	*Size of holdings*	*Pargana*	*Source*
1	Shaikh Abdul Karim and others	1658	80 *bighas*	Bahraich	Allahabad Doc. 760
2	Mir Sayyid Ahmed	1658	534 *bighas* 8 *biswas*	Bahraich	Allahabad Doc. 791
3	Shaikh Firiz	1658	58 *bighas*	Khairabad	Allahabad Doc. 876
4	Qazi Habibullah and others	1659	450 *bighas*	Sandila	NAI 1624
5	Mst. Bibi Lahari	1659	100 *bighas*	Fakhrpur	Allahabad Doc. 796
6	Mst. Chappa	1661	45 *bighas*	Sadrpur	Allahabad Doc. 762
7	Bibi Maryam	1661	80 *bighas*	Fatehpur	Allahabad Doc. 847
8	Sayyid Muhammad and others	1661	23 *bighas* 5 *biswas*	Sandila	NAI 1248
9	Bibi Jan and others	1662	2,220 *bighas*	Sailak	Allahabad Doc. 170
10	Shaikh Hisamuddin	1662	200 *bighas*	Sadrpur	Allahabad Doc. 877
11	Sayyid Muhammad Arif	1663	357 *bighas* 12 *biswas*	Bahraich	Allahabad Doc. 764
12	Shaikh Shukurullah	1664	200 *bighas*	Sailak	Allahabad Doc. 765
13	Sayyid Jamal-ud-Din and others	1664	158 *bighas* 12 *biswas*	Sailak	Allahabad Doc. 878
14	Shaikh Habibullah Khatib	1664	300 *bighas*	Gorakhpur	NAI 2165
15	Sayyid Abdul Fath	1665	10 *bighas*	Sandila	NAI 2608/8
16	Abdul Samad	1665	35 *bighas*	Sandila	NAI 2578
17	Sayyid Jamal-ud-Din	1665	267 *bighas* 19 *biswas*	Bahraich	Allahabad Doc. 797
18	Sayyid Abdul Zadir	1665	11 *bighas* 13 *biswas*	Sandila	Allahabad Doc. 3

19	Shaikh Izzatullah	1667	500 *bighas*	Lucknow	Allahabad Doc. 1190/1, 2
20	Abdul Sattar	1667	40 *bighas*	Lucknow	NAI 1658
21	Shaikh Khirz and others	1668	100 *bighas*	Sailak	Allahabad Doc. 830
22	Qazi Mubarak	1668	200 *bighas*	Sailak	NAI 1831
23	Sayyid Hasan and others	1668	135 *bighas*	Sailak	Allahabad Doc. 168
24	Shaikh Nurullah	1668	70 *bighas*	Bahraich	Allahabad Doc. 833
25	Shaikh Habibullah, Pir Muhammad and others	1669	592 *bighas*	Gorakhpur	NAI 2154
26	Shaikh Mah Mahmud	1669	240 *bighas*	Lucknow	Allahabad Doc. 204
27	Sayyid Asmatullah	1670	70 *bighas*	Sandila	Allahabad Doc. 8
28	Sayyid Muhammad	1670	50 *bighas*	Sandila	Allahabad Doc. 7
29	Mst. Mahi	1671	62 *bighas*	Bahraich	Allahabad Doc. 799
30	Qazi Wali Muhammad	1671	5,376 *bighas*	Hisampur	Allahabad Doc. 824
31	Qazi Imad-ud-Din	1671	205 *bighas* 203 *biswas*	Sandila	NAI 1772, 1381
32	Hafiz Baroz	1672	150 *bighas*	Sandila	NAI 1434
33	Mst. Fath Khatoon	1674	225 *bighas*	Gorakhpur	NAI 222
34	Sayyid Muhammad Naim and others	1674	265 *bighas*	Gorakhpur	NAI 2159
35	Mst. Shah Bibi	1674	235 *bighas*	Groakhpur	NAI 2158
36	Abdul Ali	1675	50 *bighas*	Sadrpur	Allahabad Doc. 812
37	Mst. Hafiza and Aziza Bano	1675	50 *bighas*	Sandila	NAI 2178
38	Qazi Imad-ud-Din	1675–81	above 1,000 *bighas*	Sandila	NAI 1272, 1360, 1393, 1434, 2155
39	Mir Sayyid Usman	1676	608 *bighas*	Fakhrpur	Allahabad Doc. 762
40	Sayyid Muhammad	1676	645 *bighas*	Hisampur	Allahabad Doc. 179
41	Shaikh Muhammad and others	1678	197 *bighas*	Sandila	NAI 1747

S. No.	*Name of the grantee*	*Year*	*Size of holdings*	*Pargana*	*Source*
42	Abdul Faiz	1679	680 *bighas*	Sadrpur	Allahabad Doc. 1212
43	Jafar	1679	50 *bighas*	Hisampur	Allahabad Doc. 1210
44	Muhammad Sadiq	1680	100 *bighas*	Asoha	NAI 2129
45	Bibi Niamat	1680	200 *bighas*	Khairabad	Allahabad Doc. 881
46	Sayyid Ali	1681	200 *bighas*	Hisampur	Allahabad Doc. 171
47	Mst. Rabia	1681	200 *bighas*	Gorakhpur	NAI 1388
48	Qazi Abdul Daim	1681	40 *bighas*	Sandila	NAI 1422
49	Mst. Fatima	1682	210 *bighas*	Gorakhpur	NAI 2158
50	Shaikh Abdul Badi	1682	30 *bighas*	Sandila	NAI 1344
51	Sayyid Husain and Habibullah	1682	77 *bighas*	Sailak	Allahabad Doc. 773
52	Mst. Rabia	1684	300 *bighas*	Maghar	NAI 2160
53	Sayyid Ahmed and others	1685	155 *bighas*	Fakhrpur	Allahabad Doc. 839
54	Mst. Ajaib and others	1685	150 *bighas*	Sandila	NAI 2575/15
55	Mst. Fazila and others	1685	140 *bighas*	Sandila	NAI 2578/2
56	Mst. Laidati	1685	50 *bighas*	Sadrpur	Allahabad Doc. 813
57	Shaikh Khirz and others	1685	100 *bighas*	Sailak	Allahabad Doc. 845
58	Bibi Mahi	1688	62 *bighas*	Bahraich	Allahabad Doc. 841
59	Bibi Man	1688	108 *bighas*	Bahraich	Allahabad Doc. 842
60	Sayyid Muhammad and others	1689	23 *bighas*	Sandila	NAI 1254
61	Mst. Hafiza and others	1690	400 *bighas*	Fakhrpur	Allahabad Doc. 175
62	Bibi Mubarak	1692	200 *bighas*	Hisampur	NAI 2174
63	Ziauddin	1697	194 *bighas*	Bahraich	Allahabad Doc. 1228
64	Shaikh Ghasity	1698	30 *bighas*	Sandila	NAI 1277
65	Bibi Lodhan	1697	520 *bighas*	Bahraich	Allahabad Doc. 1228
66	Mst. Hamira and others	1699	250 *bighas*	Bahraich	Allahabad Doc. 165
67	Sayyid Yahya	1700	200 *bighas*	Sailak	Allahabad Doc. 860
68	Sharafuddin	1700–1	300 *bighas*	Sandila	NAI 1305, 1755

69	Mst. Bibi Rajrabi and others	1701	190 *bighas*	Mallawan	NAI 1256
70	Sayyid Muhammad Naqi	1702	194 *bighas*	Bahraich	Allahabad Doc. 846
71	Mst. Khadiza	1702	100 *bighas*	Hisampur	Allahabad Doc. 176
72	Sayyid Faizullah	1702	790 *bighas*	Hisampur	Allahabad Doc. 173
73	Bibi Saleh	1704	200 *bighas*	Sadrpur	Allahabad Doc. 815/1, 2
74	Mst. Dilshan	1704	100 *bighas*	Hisampur	Allahabad Doc. 178
75	Mst. Jeo	1704	60 *bighas*	Khairabad	Allahabad Doc. 878
76	Fath Ali and others	1704	50 *bighas*	Sandila	NAI 2608/4
77	Mst. Parsa	1710	150 *bighas*	Sandila	NAI 1371
78	Shaikh Abul Khair and others	1715	1,860 *bighas*	Daryabad	Allahabad Doc. 32
79	Muhammad Naim and others	1716	265 *bighas*	Sandila	NAI 1652
80	Zain-ul-Abidin and others	1717	74 *bighas*	Sandila	NAI 2173
81	Sayyid Karamullah	1717	235 *bighas*	Sandila	NAI 1050
82	Shaikh Muinuddin and others	1718	15 *bighas*	Sandila	NAI 2578
83	Shaikh Khalilullah	1720	100 *bighas*	Sadrpur	Allahabad Doc. 825
84	Hafiz Abdul Ali	1721	100 *bighas*	Sandila	NAI 1389
85	Shaikh Bayazid	1728	12 *bighas*	Sandila	Allahabad Doc. 3
86	Shaikh Jalilullah	1737	50 *bighas*	Sandila	NAI 1378
87	Hafiz Muhammad Basir	1762	30 *bighas*	Sandila	NAI 1315
88	Shah Muhammad	1764	4 *bighas*	Sandila	Allahabad Doc. 439
89	Muhammad Mahali Hasan and others	1767	836 *bighas*	Hisampur	Allahabad Doc. 819
90	Sayyid Abbas	1767	305 *bighas*	Bahraich	Allahabad Doc. 824

APPENDIX III: SOME WOMEN GRANTEES OF THE SUBA

S. No.	*Name of the grantee*	*Year*	*Size of holdings*	*Pargana*	*Source*
1	Bibi Lahuri	1659	100 *bighas*	Fakhrpur	Allahabad Doc. 762
2	Mst. Chappa	1661	45 *bighas*	Khairabad	Allahabad Doc. 796
3	Bibi Maryam	1661	80 *bighas*	Fakhrpur	Allahabad Doc. 847
4	Mst. Bibi Jan and others	1662	2,220 *bighas*	Hisampur	Allahabad Doc. 169
5	Mst. Bibi Jan and others	1671	62 *bighas*	Bahraich	Allahabad Doc. 799
6	Mst. Rabia	1674	200 *bighas*	Bahraich	Allahabad Doc. 771
7	Mst. Kunzah	1674	150 *bighas*	Bahraich	Allahabad Doc. 800
8	Mst. Makhan	1674	300 *bighas*	Bahraich	Allahabad Doc. 174
9	Mst. Shah Bibi	1674	235 *bighas*	Gorakhpur	NAI 2171
10	Mst. Bibi Fath Khatoon	1674	225 *bighas*	Gorakhpur	NAI 2169
11	Mst. Hafiza and Aziza Bano	1675	90 *bighas*	Gorakhpur	NAI 2178
12	Mst. Rabia	1681	200 *bighas*	Gorakhpur	NAI 2155
13	Mst. Amina	1681	30 *bighas*	Bahraich	Allahabad Doc. 843
14	Bibi Jugi	1681	20 *bighas*	Bahraich	Allahabad Doc. 843
15	Bibi Nur	1681	20 *bighas*	Bahraich	Allahabad Doc. 843
16	Bibi Raqiah	1681	10 *bighas*	Bahraich	Allahabad Doc. 843
17	Mst. Bibi Fatima	1682	210 *bighas*	Bahraich	NAI 2158
18	Mst. Rabia	1684	300 *bighas*	Maghar	NAI 2160
19	Mst. Ajaib and others	1685	150 *bighas*	Sandila	NAI 2575/15
20	Mst. Fazila and others	1685	140 *bighas*	Sandila	NAI 2578/2
21	Mst. Laidati	1685	30 *bighas*	Khairabad	Allahabad Doc. 813
22	Bibi Kaneez and others	1691	80 *bighas*	Sadrpur	Allahabad Doc. 815/1, 2
23	Bibi Mubarak and others	1692	210 *bighas*	Hisampur	NAI 2174
24	Mst. Hafiza and others	1694	400 *bighas*	Fakhrpur	Allahabad Doc. 175
25	Mst. Hamira and others	1696	250 *bighas*	Bahraich	Allahabad Doc. 165
26	Bibi Rajrabi and others	1701	190 *bighas*	Mallawan	NAI 1256
27	Mst. Bibi Jeo	1704	100 *bighas*	Bahraich	Allahabad Doc. 807
28	Mst. Saleh and others	1704	200 *bighas*	Sadrpur	Allahabad Doc. 816/1, 2
29	Mst. Parsa	1710	150 *bighas*	Gorakhpur	NAI 1371

Bibliography

I. PRIMARY SOURCES

A. BOOKS

Abul Fazal, *Ain-i-Akbari*, vol. I, translated by H. Blochmann, Delhi, 1977.

Ain-i-Akbari, vol. II, translated by H.S. Jarret, corrected and further annotated by Sir J.N. Sarkar, Delhi, 1978.

Bernier, Francois, *Travels in Mogul Empire*, translated by A. Constable, London, 1916.

Bilgrami, Mir Ghulam Ali Azad, *Maathir-ul-Kiram*, vol. I, Lahore, 1971.

Chhabela Ram and Girdhar Lal, *Ajab-ul-Afaq*, Rotograph, Sitamau.

Husain, Shaikh Ghulam, *Sharaif-i-Usmani*, Ms. Department of History, Aligarh Muslim University, Aligarh.

Husaini, Khwaja Kamgar, *Maasir-i-Jahangiri*, ed. Azra Alavi, Delhi, 1978.

Jahangir, *Tuzuk-i-Jahangiri*, ed. Syed Ahmed Khan, Ghazeepore, 1863. English translation by A. Rogers, Delhi, 1978.

Lakhnavi, Shiv Das, *Shahnama-i-Munawwar Kalam*, Eng. trans. by Syed Hasan Askari, Patna, 1982.

Rai, Bhupat, *Insha-i-Roshan Kalam*, Kanpur, 1298 A.H.

Rai, Munshi Sahib, *Khujista-i-Kalam*, Rotograph, Raghubir Singh Collection, Sitamau.

B. DOCUMENTS

ALLAHABAD DOCUMENTS, UTTAR PRADESH STATE ARCHIVES, ALLAHABAD

S. No.	*Doc. No.*	*Year*	*Dealing with the area (pargana)*
1	3	1665	Sandila
2	7	1671	Sandila
3	8	1670	Sandila
4	9	1698	Daryabad
5	11	1728	Sandila
6	32	1732	Daryabad

S. No.	Doc. No.	Year	Dealing with the area (pargana)
7	44	1730	Mallawan
8	47	1665	Mallawan
9	55	1666	Mallawan
10	165	1690	Bahraich
11	166	1696	Bahraich
12	167	1695	Bahraich
13	168	1695	Bahraich
14	169	1668	Hisampur
15	170	1662	Sailak
16	171	1662	Hisampur
17	172	1661	Bahraich
18	173	1694	Hisampur
19	174	1702	Bahraich
20	175	1674	Fakhrpur
21	176	1690	Hisampur
22	177	1702	Hisampur
23	178	1704	Hisampur
24	179	1676	Hisampur
25	204	1669	Lucknow
26	231	1715	Sandila
27	267	1765	Amethi
28	274	1681	Sandila
29	297	1657	Sandila
30	315	1650	Sandila
31	361	1747	Sandila
32	439	1764	Sandila
33	760	1658	Bahraich
34	762	1659	Fakhrpur
35	763	1665	Bahraich
36	764	1663	Bahraich
37.	765	1665	Sailak
38	766	1676	Fakhrpur
39	767	1669	Bahraich
40	768	1669	Bahraich
41	769	1671	Bahraich
42	771	1674	Bahraich
43	772	1676	Hisampur
44	773	1682	Sailak
45	774	1682	Hisampur
46	775	1687	Sailak

S. No.	*Doc. No.*	*Year*	*Dealing with the area (pargana)*
47	776	1688	Firozabad
48	777	1700	Sadrpur
49	779	1704	Bahraich
50	781	1674	Hisampur
51	788	1674	Bahraich
52	791	1658	Bahraich
53	796	1661	Sadrpur
54	798	1666	Bahraich
55	799	1671	Bahraich
56	800	1674	Bahraich
57	801	1676	Fakharpur
58	803	1677	Sailak, Hisampur
59	804	1683	Firozabad
60	805	1687	Sailak
61	806	1697	Hisampur
62	807	1704	Bahraich
63	812	1675	Sadrpur
64	813	1685	Sadrpur
65	814	1690	Sadrpur
66	815/1, 2	1691	Sadrpur
67	816/1, 2	1704	Sadrpur
68	819	1767	Hisampur
69	822	1720	Fatehpur
70	823	1720	Sadrpur
71	824	1767	Bahraich
72	825	1715	Sadrpur
73	830	1668	Sailak
74	831	1670	Fatehpur
75	833	1665	Fatehpur
76	834	1700	Bahraich
77	836	1676	Sailak
78	837	1697	Hisampur
79	839	1685	Fakrpur
80	841	1688	Bahraich
81	842	1688	Bahraich
82	843	1688	Bahraich
83	844	1702	Bahraich
84	845	1688	Sailak
85	846	1688	Sailak
86	847	1661	Fatehpur

S. No.	Doc. No.	Year	Dealing with the area (pargana)
87	848	1664	Sailak
88	854	1724	Sadrpur
89	856	1767	Hisampur
90	857	1674	Hisampur
91	858	1677	Hisampur
92	859	1705	Bahraich
93	860	1700	Sailak
94	875	1704	Sadrpur
95	876	1658	Khairabad
96	877	1662	Sadrpur
97	878	1704	Khairabad
98	881	1680	Khariabad
99	882	1680	Khariabad
100	885	1672	Bahraich
101	892	1678	Bahraich
102	897/1, 2	1684	Bahraich
103	1187/1, 2	1663	Bahraich
104.	1189	1666	Bahraich
105	1190/1, 2	1667	Lucknow
106	1196	1672	Bahraich
107	1201	1676	Sailak, Hisampur
108	1202	1676	Sailak, Fakhrpur
109	1203	1679	Sailak, Hisampur
110	1208	1679	Hisampur
111	1210	1679	Hisampur, Fakhrpur
112	1212	1679	Bahraich
113	1216	1681	Hisampur
114	1217	1687	Bahraich
115	1219	1687	Hisampur
116	1221	1688	Hisampur
117	1222	1688	Hisampur
118	1224	1689	Hisampur
119	1228	1697	Bahraich
120	1229	1697	Bahraich
121	1230	1698	Bahraich
122	1236	1715	Hisampur
123	1237	1716	Khairabad
124	1245	1753	Sadrpur

ACQUIRED DOCUMENTS, NATIONAL ARCHIVES OF INDIA, DELHI

S. No.	*Doc. No.*	*Year*	*Dealing with the area (pargana)*
1	1050	1717	Sandila
2	1248	1661	Sandila
3	1252	1669	Lucknow
4	1254	1689	Sandila
5	1255	1697	Sandila
6	1256	1704	Mallawan
7	1267	1661	Sandila
8	1268	1662	Sandila
9	1269	1663	Sandila
10	1270	1664	Sandila
11	1272	1675	Nimkhar
12	1273	1680	Sandila
13	1277	1698	Sandila
14	1305	1700	Sandila
15	1337	1674	Sandila
16	1344	1682	Sandila
17	1345	1690	Sandila
18	1346	1698	Sandila
19	1360	1677	Sandila
20	1369	1721	Sandila
21	1370	1748	Sandila
22	1374	1679	Sandila
23	1375	1762	Sandila
24	1378	1737	Sandila
25	1379	1737	Sandila
26	1381	1671	Sandila
27	1388	1681	Sandila
28	1389	1684	Sandila
29	1391	1733	Sandila
30	1395	1681	Sandila
31	1409	1692	Sandila
32	1410	1702	Sandila
33	1414	1688	Sandila
34	1422	1681	Sandila
35	1434	1680	Sandila
36	1435	1698	Sandila
37	1436	1672	Sandila

S. No.	Doc. No.	Year	Dealing with the area (pargana)
38	1440	1689	Sandila
39	1443	1694	Sandila
40	1451	1684	Sandila
41	1473	1675	Sandila
42	1486	1664	Sandila
43	1546	1690	Sandila
44	1582	1731	Sandila
45	1620	1683	Sandila
46	1651	1684	Sandila
47	1652	1716	Sandila
48	1658	1666	Sandila
49	1742	1671	Sandila
50	1743	1673	Sandila
51	1747	1678	Sandila
52	1748	1679	Sandila
53	1755	1701	Sandila
54	2129	1680	Asoha
55	2154	1669	Gorakhpur
56	2155	1681	Gorakhpur
57	2157	1673	Gorakhpur
58	2158	1682	Gorakhpur
59	2159	1674	Gorakhpur
60	2160	1684	Gorakhpur
61	2162	1673	Gorakhpur
62	2165	1664	Gorakhpur
63	2167	1699	Gorakhpur
64	2168	1699	Gorakhpur
65	2171	1674	Gorakhpur
66	2173	1716	Gorakhpur
67	2174	1692	Hisampur
68	2178	1675	Sandila
69	2447	1716	Gorakhpur
70	2575/15	1685	Sandila
71	2578	1665	Sandila
72	2578/12	1685	Sandila
73	2578/13	1671	Sandila
74	2608	1706	Sandila
75	2608/4	1704	Sandila
76	2608/8	1665	Sandila

C. TRANSLATED AND PUBLISHED DOCUMENTS

Ansari, M.A. (ed.), *Administrative Documents of Mughal India,* Delhi, 1983.

Dutta, K.K. (ed.), *Some Mughal Farmans, Sanads and Parwanas,* Patna, 1962.

Halim, Jafar A., 'A Farman of Emperor Shahjahan', PIHRC, vol. 10.

Husain, Iqbal, 'Calendar of Khairabad Documents, from 16th to 19th century', *Islamic Culture,* 1979.

Jafri, S.Z.H., 'Two *Madad-i-Maash* Farmans from Awadh', PIHC, 1979.

Khan, Yusuf Husain (ed.), *Selected Documents of Aurangzeb's Reign,* Hyderabad, 1959.

Momin, Moinuddin, 'A *Sayurghal of* Babur', PIHC, 1961, Pt. II.

Malik, Zahiruddin, 'Documents of Muhammad Shah's Reign', *Indo-Iranica,* Calcutta, 1973.

Rashid, Abdur (ed.), *Calendar of Oriental Record,* 2 vols., Allahabad, 1959.

Saxena, Banarasi Prasad (ed.), *Calendar of Oriental Records,* vol. I, Allahabad, 1955.

Srivastava, K.P. (ed.), *Mughal Farmans (1504–1706),* Lucknow, 1974.

Tirmizi, S.A.A., *Calendar of Acquired Documents,* National Archives of India, Delhi, 1983.

Shere, S.A., 'A Farman of Shah Alam', PIHRC, vol. 20.

Some Mughal Farmans at Faizabad Museum, PIHRC, vol. 9.

Some Documents from Uttar Pradesh Government, PIHRC, 1956.

Some Documents from Uttar Pradesh State Archives, vol. 37.

Some Documents from Uttar Pradesh State Archives, vol. 38.

Some Documents Collected by Ajit Ghose, PIHRC, vol. 42.

II. SECONDARY SOURCES

Alam, Muzaffar, *The Crisis of Empire in Mughal North India: Awadh and the Punjab 1707–1748,* Delhi, 1986.

———, 'Some Aspects of the Changes in the Position of Madad-i-Maash holders in Awadh (1676–1772)', PIHC, 1974.

Ansari, M.R., *Bani-i-Dars-i-Nizami, Mulla Nizamuddin Firangi Mahali,* Aligarh, 1973.

Barnett, Richard B., *North India between Empires, Awadh, the Mughals and the British, 1720–1801,* London, 1980.

Bayly, C.A., *Rulers, Townsmen and Bazaars, North Indian Society in the Age of British Expansion, 1770–1870,* Cambridge, 1983.

Bennet, W.C., *A Report on the Family History of the Chief Clans of the Ray Bareilley District,* Lucknow, 1877.

Bilgrami, R.M., *Religious and Quasi Religious Departments of Mughal Period,* Delhi, 1984.

Bilgrami, Rafat, 'Some Mughal Revenue Grants to the Family and Khanqah of Sayyid Ashraf Jahangir', *Medieval India: A Miscellany*, 1972.

Bilgrami, Sharif-ul-Hasan, *Tarikh-i-Khat-i-Pak Bilgram*, Aligarh, 1958.

Butter, Donald, *Topography and Statistics of Southern Districts of Awadh*, edited by Safi Ahmed, Delhi, 1982.

Chandra, Satish, *Parties and Politics at Mughal Court 1704–1740*, Delhi, 1972.

District Gazetteers: Bahraich, Basti, Ballia, Gonda, Faizabad, Lucknow, Gorakhpur, Sultanpur, edited by H.R. Nevill.

Eaton, Richard M., 'The Court and Dargah in 17th Century Deccan', *IESHR*, vol. 10, 1973.

———, *Sufis of Bijapur, 1300–1700*, New Jersey, 1978.

Elliot, C.A., *Chronicles of Oanao*, Allahabad, 1862.

Frye, R.N. (ed.), *The Cambridge History of Iran*, vol. 4, Cambridge, 1975.

Grewal, J.S., *Miscellaneous Articles*, Amritsar, 1974.

Grewal, J.S. and B.N. Goswamy, *The Mughals, Sikh Rulers and Vaishnavas of Pindori*, Simla, 1969.

———, *The Mughal and Jogis of Jakhbar*, Simla, 1967.

Gilani, Manzar Hasan, *Hindustan Mein Musalmano ka Nizam-i-Taalim*, Delhi, 1966.

Grover, B.R., 'Presidential Address', *Medieval Section*, PIHC, 1976.

Hai, Maulana Hakim Sayyid Abdul, *Islami Ulum-o-Funun Hindustan Mein*, Azamgarh, 1969.

Habib, Irfan, *Agrarian System of Mughal India*, Bombay, 1963.

———, *An Atlas of the Mughal Empire*, 1982.

Hasan, Ibn, *Central Structure of Mughal Empire*, Delhi, 1970.

Hasan, Nurul, *Some Thoughts on Agrarian Relation in Mughal India*, Delhi, 1973.

Husain, Iqbal, '*Madad-i-Maash* Regulation in the Mughal Empire', PIHC, 1977.

Husain, S.M. Azizuddin, '*Kalimat-i-Aurangzeb*: A Source of Aurangzeb's Reign', PIHC, 1979.

Irwine, W.C., *The Garden of India*, vol. I, Lucknow, 1973.

Jafar, S.M., *Education in Muslim India*, Delhi, 1972.

Jafri, S.Z.H., 'Two Madad-i-Maash Farmans of Aurangzeb's Reign from Awadh', PIHC, 1979.

Jha, D.N., 'Temples as Landed Magnets in Early Medieval South India', in R.S. Sharma and V. Jha (eds.), *Indian Society, Historical Probings*, Delhi, 1974.

Khan, Iqtedar Alam, 'The Nobility Under Akbar and Development of His Religious Policy (1560–80)', *Journal of the Royal Asiatic Society*, 1958.

Law, N.N., *Promotion of Learning in India During Mohammedan Rule*, London, 1916.

Malik, Zahiruddin, *The Reign Muhammad Shah* (*1719–1748*), 1977.

Moreland, W.H., *Agrarian System of Muslim India,* Delhi, 1968.
Moosvi, Shireen, '*Sayurghal* Statistics in the *Ain-i-Akbari*: An Analysis', *IHR,* 1976.
Nizami, K.A., *Studies in Medieval Indian Society,* Allahabad, 1966.
Parsad, Durga, *Tarikh-i-Sandila,* Lucknow, 1916.
Rashid, Abdur, *Society and Culture in Medieval India,* Calcutta, 1969.
Rashid, Shaikh Abdur, '*Sayurghal* Lands Under the Mughals', in H.R. Gupta (ed.), *Essays Presented to Sir J.N. Sarkar,* Hoshiarpur, 1958.
Rizvi, S.A.A., *Shah Waliullah and His Times,* Canberra, 1980.
Sarkar, Jagdish Narayan, *A study of 18th century India,* vol. I, Calcutta, 1976.
Sarkar, Sir J.N., *India of Aurangzeb's Reign,* Calcutta, 1901.
———, *Studies in Aurangzeb's Reign,* Calcutta, 1933.
———, *Mughal Administration,* Calcutta, 1963.
———, *Short History of Aurangzeb's Reign,* Calcutta, 1962.
Siddiqui, I.H., 'Wajh-i-Maash Grants Under the Afghan Kings (1451–1555)', *Medieval India: A Miscellany,* vol. II, Bombay, 1972.
Siddiqui, N.A., *Land Revenue Administration Under the Mughals (1700–1750),* Bombay, 1970.
———,'Pulls and Pressures on the Faujdar Under the Mughals', PIHC, 1967.
Sinha, S.N., *Suba of Allahabad Under the Great Mughals,* Delhi, 1974.
Sharar, Abdul Halim, *Lucknow*: *The Last Phase of an Oriental Culture,* translated and edited by E.S. Harcourt and Fakhir Hussain, London, 1975.
Srivastava, A.L., *First two Nawabs of Awadh,* Agra, 1954.
Sharma, R.S., *Aspects of Political Ideas and Institutions in Ancient India,* Delhi, 1968.
Tripathi, R.P., *Some Aspects of Muslim Administration,* Allahabad, 1964.
———, *Rise and Fall of the Mughal Empire,* Allahabad, 1972.
Thapar, Romila, 'Social Mobility in Ancient India', in R.S Sharma and V. Jha (eds.), *Indian Society, Historical Probings,* Delhi, 1974.
Tirmizi, S.A.T., *Edicts from Mughal Harem,* Delhi, 1979.

Index